# PRAY
## LIKE THIS

*Living the
Lord's Prayer*

# STEVE GAINES

LifeWay Press®
Nashville, Tennessee

ISBN 978-1-4627-4288-2 • Item 005793411

Dewey decimal classification: 226.96
Subject headings: LORD'S PRAYER \ JESUS CHRIST—PRAYERS \ PRAYER

Scripture quotations are taken from the Christian Standard Bible®, Copyright © 2017 by Holman Bible Publishers. Used by permission. Christian Standard Bible® and CSB® are federally registered trademarks of Holman Bible Publishers.

To order additional copies of this resource, write to LifeWay Resources Customer Service; One LifeWay Plaza; Nashville, TN 37234; fax 615-251-5933; phone toll free 800-458-2772; order online at LifeWay.com; email orderentry@lifeway.com; or visit the LifeWay Christian Store serving you.

*Printed in the United States of America*

Groups Ministry Publishing • LifeWay Resources • One LifeWay Plaza • Nashville, TN 37234

# Contents

# About the Author

## Steve Gaines

Steve Gaines serves as the senior pastor of Bellevue Baptist Church in Memphis, Tennessee, and currently serves as the president of the Southern Baptist Convention. He has served in four churches as senior pastor over the past thirty years. He holds a PhD in preaching from Southwestern Baptist Theological Seminary in Forth Worth, Texas. Steve and his wife, Donna, have four children: Grant, Lindsey, Allison, and Bethany. Steve and Donna are both authors. Steve has published a musical worship CD, and his latest books include *Pray like it Matters, Share Jesus like it Matters,* and a rerelease of his devotional book *Morning Manna.*

## Michael Kelley

Michael helped develop the content for this Bible study. He lives in Nashville, Tennessee, with his wife, Jana, and three children: Joshua, Andi, and Christian. He serves as the director of Groups Ministry for LifeWay Christian Resources. As a communicator, Michael speaks across the country at churches, conferences, and retreats. He's the author of *Wednesdays Were Pretty Normal: A Boy, Cancer, and God; Transformational Discipleship;* and *Boring: Finding an Extraordinary God in an Ordinary Life.*

# Introduction

Jesus was a prayer warrior. Although He was the Son of God, He recognized the necessity of constantly abiding in a relationship of dependency on His Father. His disciples, noticing Jesus' habit of seeking time alone with the Father, requested, "Lord, teach us to pray, just as John also taught his disciples" (Luke 11:1). Jesus' response, as recorded by Matthew, was both simple and profound, both practical and deeply spiritual:

> Our Father in heaven,
> your name be honored as holy.
> Your kingdom come.
> Your will be done
> on earth as it is in heaven.
> Give us today our daily bread.
> And forgive us our debts,
> as we also have forgiven our debtors.
> And do not bring us into temptation,
> but deliver us from the evil one.
> **MATTHEW 6:9-13**

The Lord's Prayer, as it's known today, is one of the most familiar passages in Scripture. Yet far too many Christians, caught up in the rush of daily life, don't make time to pray. In failing to follow Jesus' example, they're neglecting a discipline that's absolutely critical to an intimate, growing relationship with God.

*Pray like This* takes a fresh look at each phrase in the Lord's Prayer to reveal its meaning and its implications for our prayer lives and our daily lives. We'll understand the significance of calling on God as Father, honoring His holy name, seeking His kingdom and His will, acknowledging our dependence on Him for every daily need, forgiving other people as He has forgiven us, and relying on His protection and deliverance from evil.

Following Jesus' Model Prayer will lead us to fall more in love with our Heavenly Father and grow in our desire to engage in conversation with Him. As we study and apply Jesus' words, may we develop a more vibrant prayer life that leads to worship, spiritual maturity, dependence on God, and a knowledge of His will.

# How to Use This Study

This Bible study provides a guided process for individuals and small groups to explore Jesus' Model Prayer in Matthew 6 and to apply it to their prayer lives. This study follows a six-week format that examines these topics:

**WEEK 1**
The Fatherhood of God

**WEEK 2**
The Worthiness of God

**WEEK 3**
The Kingdom and Will of God

**WEEK 4**
The Provision of God

**WEEK 5**
The Forgiveness of God

**WEEK 6**
The Protection of God

Each week is divided into five days of personal study. In these studies you'll find biblical teaching and interactive questions that will help you understand and apply the Lord's Prayer to your relationship with your Heavenly Father.

In addition to the personal study, six group sessions are provided that are designed to spark conversations based on brief video teachings. Each group session is divided into three sections:

1. **"START"** focuses participants on the topic of the session's video teaching.
2. **"WATCH"** provides key ideas presented in the video and space to take notes.
3. **"DISCUSS"** guides the group to respond to and apply the video teaching.

# Tips for Leading a Group

## Prayerfully Prepare

Prepare for each group session with prayer. Ask the Holy Spirit to work through you and the group discussion as you point to Jesus each week through God's Word.

**REVIEW** the weekly material and group questions ahead of time.

**PRAY** for each person in the group.

## Minimize Distractions

Do everything in your ability to help people focus on what's most important:

**CONNECT** with God, with the Bible, and with one another.

Create a comfortable environment. If group members are uncomfortable, they'll be distracted and therefore not engaged in the group experience.

**CONSIDER** seating, temperature, lighting, refreshments, surrounding noise,and general cleanliness.

At best, thoughtfulness and hospitality show guests and group members they're welcome and valued in whatever environment you choose to gather. At worst, people may never notice your effort, but they're also not distracted.

# Include Others

Your goal is to foster a community in which people are welcome just as they are but encouraged to grow spiritually. Always be aware of opportunities to include and invite.

**INCLUDE** anyone who visits the group.

**INVITE** new people to join your group.

# Encourage Discussion

A good small-group experience has the following characteristics.

**EVERYONE PARTICIPATES.** Encourage everyone to ask questions, share responses, or read aloud.

**NO ONE DOMINATES—NOT EVEN THE LEADER.** Be sure your time speaking as a leader takes up less than half your time together as a group. Politely guide discussion if anyone dominates.

**NOBODY IS RUSHED THROUGH QUESTIONS.** Don't feel that a moment of silence is a bad thing. People often need time to think about their responses to questions they've just heard or to gain courage to share what God is stirring in their hearts.

**INPUT IS AFFIRMED AND FOLLOWED UP.** Make sure you point out something true or helpful in a response. Don't just move on. Build community with follow-up questions, asking how other people have experienced similar things or how a truth has shaped their understanding of God and the Scripture you're studying. People are less likely to speak up if they fear that you don't actually want to hear their answers or that you're looking for only a certain answer.

**GOD AND HIS WORD ARE CENTRAL.** Opinions and experiences can be helpful, but God has given us the truth. Trust Scripture to be the authority and God's Spirit to work in people's lives. You can't change anyone, but God can. Continually point people to the Word and to active steps of faith.

# Keep Connecting

Think of ways to connect with group members during the week. Participation during the group session is always improved when members spend time connecting with one another outside the group sessions. The more people are comfortable with and involved in one another's lives, the more they'll look forward to being together. When people move beyond being friendly to truly being friends who form a community, they come to each session eager to engage instead of merely attending.

**ENCOURAGE** group members with thoughts, commitments, or questions from the session by connecting through emails, texts, and social media.

**BUILD** deeper friendships by planning or spontaneously inviting group members to join you outside your regularly scheduled group time for meals; fun activities; and projects around your home, church, or community.

# THE FATHERHOOD OF GOD

# *START*

Welcome to group session 1 of *Pray like This.* Ask participants to introduce themselves by giving quick answers to the following questions.

**What's your name, and what brought you to this group?**

**What's one word you would use to describe your prayer life?**

**If you could make your prayer life different in one way, what would it be?**

Prayer is a subject that is or should be close to the core of every Christian's walk with God. Despite that, many of us live with a sense of longing when we think about our prayer lives. We know we ought to pray, we might even desire to pray with greater fervency, yet we aren't growing in our capacity for and joy in prayer.

In Matthew 6:9-13 Jesus taught us what we need to know about prayer. When His closest followers asked Him to teach them to pray, He answered with the Model Prayer, a text that still instructs Christ followers today in the discipline of talking and listening to God.

Over the next six weeks your group will examine this Model Prayer line by line, each week growing in your understanding and practice of prayer. Together you'll learn from Jesus to "pray like this" (v. 9) so that you can grow in intimacy with your Heavenly Father.

**Read together the text of Jesus' Model Prayer, found in Matthew 6:9-13. Then watch video session 1.**

# WATCH

Through grace and faith in Christ, not only does He bring us into His kingdom; He brings us into His family, and we are now His adopted sons and daughters.

Jesus said, "I want you to do more than call Him Father. I want you to call Him Papa, Abba."

Ultimately, what drives our worship, what drives our intimacy with God, is the sense of Him being Father.

It's only through Christ and the gospel that we actually come into a Father-child relationship with the Lord. Father is the Christian name for God.

When you connect with God as Father, you're looking for two things:
1. Protection   2. Provision

God is the perfect Father. That's why we can go into the throne room through Jesus Christ and say, "Abba, Father."

The Model Prayer starts with "our Father," not just "my Father." The church is a family. He's the Father of our church, of our family.

Feelings never drive our faith. It's the facts of the Word of God.

God is an intimate, loving, caring, long-suffering Father who desires a relationship with us.

When I start my prayer with "Father God" or "God the Father," that reminds me that He delights in me, that He welcomes me into His family, that I'm adopted.

Once we know the Father through His Son, Jesus Christ, we can go to Him anywhere, anytime, about anything in life.

When people take prayer casually, it shows they don't really understand the intimacy and the cost.

# DISCUSS

The first line of Jesus' Model Prayer reads, "Our Father in heaven ..." (Matt. 6:9).

> **What's one insight in the video that challenged you?**
>
> **Why is it essential for our prayers to begin by acknowledging God as our Father?**
>
> **Is acknowledging God as your Father difficult for you? Why or why not?**

Jesus began His Model Prayer with a very intimate title for God. In doing so, Jesus reminded us that we, as Christians, have an intimate relationship with God. Yet many believers might have trouble addressing God this way because of past experiences with our earthly fathers. Acknowledging God as our Father reminds us that regardless of who our earthly fathers are or were, we have a Heavenly Father who loves, provides for, and plans good for us.

> **When we call God Father in prayer, what are we communicating about ourselves?**
>
> **How can remembering that we're God's adopted children change the way we pray?**
>
> **Read Hebrews 4:16. How does knowing that God is your Father give you confidence to approach Him in prayer?**

If God is our Father, we're His adopted children because of the gospel. Therefore, we can come freely and boldly into His presence, knowing He won't turn us away.

## PRAY

*Thank the Lord for being your Father. Ask Him to help any group members who have difficulty relating to Him as Father to accept by faith His love and care for them.*

# DAY 1
## The Adopted Children

**Read Ephesians 1:3-14.**

What does the word *father* mean to you? Depending on your past, it might bring to mind images of care and protection. Conversely, it could bring up feelings of neglect and bitterness. Joy, anger, rejection, affection—all these emotions are packed into the single word *father*. This is the word Jesus used to begin the Model Prayer:

> You should pray like this:
> Our Father in heaven.
> **MATTHEW 6:9**

The starting point for approaching God as Christ followers is summed up in this single word: *Father*. Because that word is loaded with preconceived notions for all of us, depending on our relationships with our earthly fathers, praying in this way can be either extraordinarily comforting or extraordinarily problematic. Part of our growth in Christ, as well as our growth in prayer, involves recovering the meaning of this word as it's applied to God.

What does it mean to call God Father? It means, first and foremost, recognizing that addressing God like this in prayer is a unique privilege for Christians. Because all of us have been born in sin, we're separated from our holy God. Far from being our Father, we're His enemies—opposed to Him—for in our sin we would much rather live under our own authority than His.

But when we believe the gospel, He who was once our enemy becomes our Father. We who were once orphans are brought into God's family. Because of the sacrifice of Jesus and our belief in Him, we have a place at God's table.

The astounding reality for Christians is that our adoption by God doesn't have an expiration date. Once adopted, we're forever His children, and as Paul would say in Ephesians 1:3, God has given us "every spiritual blessing in the heavens." As our Father, God has held nothing back from us, because He has given us everything in Jesus Christ.

This is why Jesus wants us to begin our prayers with the word *Father*. When we do, we remind ourselves that God has made a way for us to be in His family.

We remind ourselves of His abiding love and care. We confess that no matter what the circumstances might be in our lives, He's with us and for us. Regardless of what we've experienced from our earthly fathers, God is redeeming that word for us. So we can come to Him over and over again, knowing that He's indeed our Father.

**Are there any obstacles to your calling God Father in prayer? What are they?**

**Why is it significant to you today to remember that you're God's adopted child?**

**How does remembering that fact change the way you pray?**

## PRAY

*Embrace the great joy and privilege of calling God Father. Using Ephesians 1:3-14 as a guide, thank Him specifically for the cosmic benefits of being His adopted child.*

# DAY 2
## The Loving Father

**Read 1 John 3:1-2.**

When Jesus told His first followers to address God as Father, it must have come as a shock. It wasn't the first shocking thing He had said to them, for this Model Prayer comes in the context of Jesus' great Sermon on the Mount.

Jesus had warmed up the crowd with controversial statements about what it really means to be called blessed and with the assertion that thinking badly of people is the same as killing them. But the introduction of the word *Father* took the sermon to another level.

Judaism strongly held to the established belief that God was absolutely unapproachable. Was He to be loved? Certainly. Respected? Absolutely. Feared? Without question. This was the culture that wouldn't even speak the revealed name of God, and when people had to write it in Scripture, they did so with great honor and respect. Some traditions say scribes broke the pens they had used to write the name of God after they had finished.

Enter Jesus, this strange rabbi who had no fear of or regard for the religious leaders of the time and who spoke with unmatched authority. There He was on a hillside talking about the revered God of Israel with an air of unmistakable familiarity. And that's just what God was going for.

God's purpose wasn't to be disrespected or approached casually—far from it. It was that God wanted to be in a relationship with His people that wasn't marked by fear but by love, not by apprehension but by an appreciation of His great grace and compassion. He wanted to be their dad.

That's where the love of God takes us. John described it like this: "See what great love the Father has given us that we should be called God's children" (1 John 3:1). God's great love doesn't make us His servants. It doesn't make us the people He puts up with. God's great love makes us His sons and daughters. *Father* is the Christian name for God.

A real father cares. He protects. He encourages. He advises. But above all, a real father loves. Always and without condition. A real father waits on the porch to welcome home his children, regardless of where they've been or what they've done. A real father is proud of his children and takes no greater pleasure than giving them what they need.

God has such an intense desire for fatherhood that He's willing, day in and day out, to adopt spiritual orphans from the world into his family. *Father* isn't a universal term for God, for not every human being is a child of God. God's family has only one natural child, and that's Jesus Christ. Everyone else comes into the family by adoption. God has brought us into His house, never to be put out in the cold again. That's what a real father does.

**Why is it crucial to embrace God as Father when you pray?**

**What might your prayers sound like if you didn't see God as a loving Father?**

**What are some ways you can embrace God's loving fatherhood without treating Him flippantly or casually?**

## PRAY

*Ask God to help you recall tangible examples of His fatherhood from the past few days. As you name them in prayer, thank your Father for His love and care.*

# DAY 3
## The Spirit Who Reminds

**Read Romans 8:14-16.**

It's amazing and miraculous to think that we, as sinful humans, can know God as our Father. This reality could be accomplished only by the death and resurrection of Jesus Christ. Because of the gospel, we now know God as Father, and He relates to us as His beloved children.

God is very concerned that we understand and remember the nature of our relationship with Him. For this reason one of the primary functions of the Holy Spirit is to remind us of the reality of our Father's closeness:

> All those led by God's Spirit are God's sons. You did not receive a spirit of slavery to fall back into fear. Instead, you received the Spirit of adoption, by whom we cry out, *"Abba,* Father!" The Spirit himself testifies together with our spirit that we are God's children.
> **ROMANS 8:14-16**

This function of the Holy Spirit is very different from the one many of us tend to think of. Many of us think of the Spirit of God as the voice in our heads that constantly tells us to stop doing what we know is wrong or to start doing more of what we know is right. We think of Him as the source of the refrain of guilt inside our heads saying either "No! No! No!" or "More! More! More!"

While the Holy Spirit of God lives inside us to convict us of sin and righteousness, another big role is to remind us of our true identity. He's there to whisper to us over and over, "You're a child of God. He's your Father." The word *Abba* points to the familiarity and intimacy God wants us to experience with Him. It's a term of closeness. It's a term of love. It's not just Father; it's Daddy. And let's be honest: we need that reminder.

We need to be reminded of God's fatherhood because of our overwhelming tendency to look at our circumstances and doubt whether it's true. We struggle financially. We undergo chemotherapy. We can't seem to overcome sin. We're tired and poor and unfaithful. And because we are, we often forget that God is our Father. So the Holy Spirit reminds us again and again. He reminds us when we're in pain. He reminds us when we're self-reliant. He reminds us when we're in the throes of temptation. Time and again comes the echo of the Spirit in our hearts: "You're a child of God."

**Read Romans 8:14-16 again. Do you typically think of the Holy Spirit as having this function—to remind you that you're a child of God? Why or why not?**

**How does knowing that you're a child of God change the way you think about and relate to God's Spirit?**

**How does knowing that God wants you to relate to Him as your Father give you confidence to pray today?**

## PRAY

*Ask the Holy Spirit to remind you that God is your Father and that you're His child. Remember this truth as you let Him quiet your heart and your mind. Then pray in confidence because your Father hears your prayer.*

# DAY 4
## The Father Who's Right

**Read Matthew 7:9-11.**

When we reach out to God as our Father, we recognize that certain realities are baked into that designation. When we call God Father, we're implicitly saying He's loving. We're also saying He's a provider. We're saying He's wise. These are characteristics that all fathers—and certainly our Heavenly Father—should embody.

But all fathers other than God fall short in all these attributes. They may want to be perfectly loving, they may strive to be faithful providers, and they may aspire to be perfectly wise, but fathers, like the rest of us, are broken people. Despite their best efforts, they always fall short. But not God.

God is the Father who always makes right decisions. In Matthew 7 Jesus not only pointed out the difference between God and our earthly fathers, but He also used that difference to give us confidence in our prayers:

> Who among you, if his son asks him for bread, will give him a stone?
> Or if he asks for a fish, will give him a snake? If you then, who are
> evil, know how to give good gifts to your children, how much more
> will your Father in heaven give good things to those who ask him.
> **MATTHEW 7:9-11**

Jesus' point was that God knows what He's doing, and He's generous. But by implication Jesus was also saying our good Father knows, better than we do, the difference between a fish and a snake. That's important because often we don't. For example, we might come to God in prayer asking for something. What we're asking for might be, in our view, the best thing for us. But because God is perfect in His wisdom and fatherhood, He knows there's another side to what we're asking for that will actually harm us. In other words, we might think we're asking for a fish when we're really asking for a snake. We might think we're asking for bread when we're really asking for a stone.

To approach God as Father is to acknowledge that He knows what's best for us. He isn't content to be our butler, simply giving what we ask for when we ask for it. He's a good Father who not only knows the difference between a fish and a snake and between bread and a stone but is also so committed to our good that He will give us what's best. And He will do so even when we might not realize that what He's giving us is exactly what we need.

Describe a time when God didn't answer your prayer the way you thought He should, but in the end His answer was for your benefit.

How does recalling that experience give you confidence in God as your Father?

How might you pray differently when you're convinced that your Father's decisions are always right?

## PRAY

*Begin by thanking God for His wisdom and generosity. As you think about the time when God answered your prayer in a different way than you thought He should, confess your inability to know what's best. Then express your confidence in Him as your Father, telling Him that all His ways and decisions are right.*

## DAY 5
# The Celebration of Children

**Read Zephaniah 3:14-17.**

If God is our Father, then we're His children. This is a wondrous reality, one the children of God should never get over. It's even more amazing to realize that God doesn't reluctantly hear from His children but instead lovingly and enthusiastically welcomes us into His presence.

This truth highlights another difference between our Heavenly Father and our earthly fathers. Though our fathers might be good and faithful men who strive to love, provide for, and protect their children, they're also still men. Because they are, they grow tired and weary. Surely every father shares the experience of having been so tired after a long day at work that he didn't have the energy to laugh, play with, and spend quality time with his children.

But not God. The prophet Zephaniah described God's posture toward His children in wonderful detail:

> Sing for joy, Daughter Zion;
> shout loudly, Israel!
> Be glad and celebrate with all your heart,
> Daughter Jerusalem!
> The LORD has removed your punishment;
> he has turned back your enemy.
> The King of Israel, the LORD, is among you;
> you need no longer fear harm.
> On that day it will be said to Jerusalem:
> "Do not fear;
> Zion, do not let your hands grow weak.
> The LORD your God is among you,
> a warrior who saves.
> He will rejoice over you with gladness.
> He will be quiet in his love.
> He will delight in you with singing."
> **ZEPHANIAH 3:14-17**

The prophet began with an exhortation for the children of God to sing and shout with joy and not to hold back in their celebration. Why? Because God had removed their punishment. Though these words were originally applicable to God's discipline of His people in the Old Testament, they're also gloriously true of people today who've believed the gospel.

The ultimate source of our ongoing, everlasting joy is that God has removed our guilt and shame through the sacrifice of Jesus. In doing so, He has also overcome our last and greatest enemy—death.

God isn't ashamed for us to call Him our Father; indeed, He celebrates over His children with gladness. He exuberantly welcomes us into His presence time and time again, and no matter how much joy we might feel there, it doesn't compare to the amount of joy He feels.

Consider that for a moment. For a child of God, coming to the Lord in prayer is an opportunity to join God in a celebration. Though we might come to prayer with a heavy heart, burdened by serious trouble, disease, or discouragement, we find our Father waiting there who's exceedingly glad to welcome us into His presence.

**Do you have trouble believing God is excited to meet with you in prayer? Why or why not?**

**What obstacles keep you from seeing prayer as a celebration with your Father?**

**What are some specific ways you can celebrate the reality of the gospel before, during, and after your prayers?**

## PRAY

*Even now God is rejoicing over you with singing. Keep that thought in your mind as you enter His presence and join Him in the celebration. Celebrate the Father as He celebrates His children. To begin, consider singing a song of celebration to the Lord.*

# THE WORTHINESS OF GOD

# *START*

Welcome to group session 2 of *Pray like This*. Ask participants to discuss what they learned in their personal study by answering the following questions.

**What's one truth that stood out to you as you completed the personal study this week?**

**Based on your study, why is it essential for us to begin our prayers by acknowledging that God is our Father?**

The second line of Jesus' Model Prayer is "Your name be honored as holy" (Matt. 6:9).

**What image comes to your mind when you think of the word *holy*?**

Having addressed God as Father, Jesus moves us deeper into prayer by asking the Lord for His name to be honored as holy. This part of Jesus' prayer challenges our priorities and desires by rightly prioritizing God and His glory above anything else.

The Christian life should be centered on the glory of God more than on our personal needs. In this video we'll dig more deeply into the name and glory of God to learn how a desire for God's renown should characterize our lives.

**Read together the text of Jesus' Model Prayer, found in Matthew 6:9-13. Then watch video session 2.**

# WATCH

Prayer is about God and His glory, not about us and our needs.

When you begin by focusing on God, it fuels the rest of your prayer life.

Worship is critical to prayer.

The names of God reflect His character.

We manifest and bear His name. That's the way He honors His name in our world today—through our life, our behavior, and our attitudes.

There's something special about the name of God. Everywhere His name goes, His presence goes.

Everywhere His name is honored, His name is hallowed, His name is lifted up nonstop, He's there in the midst. There's something powerful about the name of our God.

For us to declare God's holiness is to acknowledge who He is.

It is when I have found the surrender and the posture of submission that come from saying, "God, You are holy" that I am in a safe place to begin to pray the other requests.

Praying to God as your Father and then saying, "God, You are holy" immediately puts prayer as a God-centered exercise.

Start with remembering. Start with gratitude.

When you move into adoration, that's really all about who He is.

When we grow in our knowledge of God through prayer or Bible study— the more we know Him—the more we will adore Him.

# DISCUSS

**What's one insight in the video that challenged you?**

**Did any of the video teaching change your understanding of why you should pray for God's name to be honored as holy?**

**What are possible obstacles to your truly desiring the name of God to be regarded as holy?**

This second line of Jesus' Model Prayer reminds us that the true focus of prayer isn't us; it's God and His glory. Even the personal requests we make in prayer are all granted with God's glory in mind. Our prayers must reflect the fact that our greatest desire is for God's name to be known and honored in the world.

**Think about your prayer life. Is it more centered on God or yourself? Why?**

**What are some practical ways you can adjust your prayer life to be more God-centered?**

**How do you think your perspective on the circumstances of life would be different if your greatest desire was for God to be known and glorified?**

Our prayers often reveal where our true priorities lie. If we're praying primarily for our own comfort or our own needs, we're likely focused on ourselves. But if our prayers reveal a desire for God's name and glory to be lifted up, we're following Jesus down the road of self-denial.

# PRAY

*Lead the group in prayer. Ask each group member to praise God for one of His specific attributes. Then close the prayer by asking the Lord to make known His great name and glory throughout the earth.*

# DAY 1
## *The Revealed Name*

**Read Exodus 3:1-15.**

Jesus began His Model Prayer by reminding His followers to address God as Father. This is the unique privilege of Christians—those who've been made children of God by His grace through Jesus' death and resurrection. But then Jesus continued with the first request in the Model Prayer: "Your name be honored as holy" (Matt. 6:9). We should pray that God's name will be honored as holy.

If this request sounds strange to us, it might be because we tend to place less significance on names than people did in biblical times. For us, the name of a person, place, or thing is simply a designation, an identifying label. But when the Bible speaks of a name, it means something much deeper. A name is a one-word summation of the essence of the person, place, or thing. A person's name is therefore a summary of his or her character.

Hundreds of years before Jesus gave us this Model Prayer, Moses met with God and had a conversation that centered on the subject of names. Moses had seen a bush that was on fire but didn't burn up. When he approached the bush, the voice of God told him that he was on holy ground. Then that same voice told him to go to the Egyptians who had enslaved God's people and demand that they let the Israelites go. In response Moses introduced the subject of names:

> Moses asked God, "If I go to the Israelites and say to them,
> 'The God of your fathers has sent me to you,' and they ask
> me, 'What is his name?' what should I tell them?"
> **EXODUS 3:13**

Moses wasn't necessarily asking for a secret name of God so that the people would know God had really sent him. Instead, he was asking, "Who are You really?" It's a valid question. After all, Moses had been in the desert for forty years with no communication from God. And that's not to mention the dire circumstances of God's chosen people. Though God had promised them a land of their own and deliverance, they had been trapped in backbreaking slavery for four hundred years. Doesn't it make sense that they would look up to the heavens with outstretched hands and say, "Are You there? Do You care? If so, where are You?"

God responded like this: "I AM WHO I AM. This is what you are to say to the Israelites: I AM has sent me to you" (Ex. 3:14). God's name, as revealed to Moses, doesn't sound much like a name at all; in fact, it's a form of the verb *to be*. It might literally be translated, "I am the One who always is."

Moses was struggling with his situation. And he came from a struggling people that had been enslaved for four hundred years. If God is the One who always is, He's invested in the present. He wasn't just telling the Israelites to look to the future or remember the past. He's the God of right now. He was there with His people in their bondage. He felt their backbreaking labor. He remained with them in their suffering (see Ex. 2:23-25; 3:7-10).

**Read Nehemiah 9:9-21, an excerpt from a prayer Nehemiah recorded about God's provision and presence with the Israelites in the wilderness. Then record what most captures your attention in this prayer.**

God has given Christians another name by which we can know Him: Immanuel, which means "God is with us" (Matt. 1:23).

**Is it ever difficult for you to believe God is truly with you in your struggles? When?**

**When you don't feel God's presence as you pray, how do you battle doubt that He cares about you?**

**How does knowing God is truly with us in the present shape the way we pray?**

## PRAY

*As you pray today, thank God that we can know Him by His names I AM and Immanuel. Ask Him to make you aware that He's present with you and cares about your feelings and your struggles. Allow that knowledge to permeate the way you pray about specific situations and needs in your life today.*

# DAY 2
## *The Holy Name*

**Read Isaiah 6:1-8.**

Jesus said we should pray that God's name—His identity and character—will be honored as holy. Our desire in prayer, first and foremost, should be for the world to understand and honor who God is and what He has done.

When we pray for all people everywhere to honor God's name as holy, we're joining a call to worship God that even now is ringing in the heavens. That's what Isaiah encountered as he was taken up in a vision and saw the Lord:

> In the year that King Uzziah died, I saw the Lord seated on a high and lofty throne, and the hem of his robe filled the temple. Seraphim were standing above him; they each had six wings: with two they covered their faces, with two they covered their feet, and with two they flew. And one called to another:
> Holy, holy, holy is the LORD of Armies;
> his glory fills the whole earth.
>
> **ISAIAH 6:1-3**

Can you imagine the scene? Let's not miss the significance that Isaiah "saw the Lord" (v. 1). That, in and of itself, is amazing, since Isaiah and his people firmly believed it was impossible to see the Lord and live. Even Moses, who related to God intimately, saw only the backside of the Lord as He passed by. But Isaiah was taken into the very throne room, face-to-face with the Almighty.

The creatures attending in the throne room issued a very distinctive call to praise. Their words echoed through the halls of eternity: "Holy, holy, holy" (v. 3). In Hebrew the number 3 conveys completeness or wholeness, it signifies what's real and perfect, and it's the number of the divine. By calling God holy three times, the seraphim pointed to the essential, foundational nature of God's holiness. They didn't chant, "Loving, loving, loving" or even "Glorious, glorious, glorious." They emphasized God's holiness. We too must start with this charac-teristic if we want to understand who God is.

To be holy is to be separate. Other. Apart. When we describe God as holy, the word sums up everything that makes Him who He is and sets Him apart from us. But this word is more than a characteristic of God; it summarizes all of His characteristics. Therefore, His holiness filters down into everything else we say about Him.

God's love is a holy love. His justice is a holy justice. His wrath is a holy wrath. God's holiness reminds us that God is completely and perfectly pure, without spot or blemish. God is wholly other—different and set apart from us. Jesus said we're to pray that the entire world comes to this recognition. This overarching desire frames the way we continue our prayer.

**How would you describe God's holiness in your own words?**

**How should acknowledging God's holiness change the way you approach Him in prayer?**

**Reflect on your prayer life over the past several weeks. How strongly does your prayer life reflect a desire for God's name to be regarded as holy?**

## PRAY

*Confess to the Lord that you desire greater zeal for His name to be regarded as holy. Even as you pray for His name to be recognized as holy throughout the earth, also pray that God will help you honor and revere His holiness in your own life.*

# DAY 3
## The Glorious Name

**Read Isaiah 48:10-11.**

Jesus taught that as His followers pray, our priority should be the recognition and reverence of God's name in the whole earth. Although we might grow in our commitment to this aim even as we pray for it, we can also be assured that God Himself is committed to the glory of His own name throughout the world.

The pages of Scripture are replete with acknowledgments of the glory of God and exhortations to glorify Him. That's the theme of the second half of the seraphim's song in Isaiah 6:

> Holy, holy, holy is the LORD of Armies;
> his glory fills the whole earth.
> **ISAIAH 6:3**

The writings of prophets like Habakkuk reveal a longing for the world to be filled with the glory of the Lord (see Hab. 2:14). God refused to share His glory or praise with idols in passages like Isaiah 42:8. In fact, the glory of the Lord was a tangible reality in certain sections of the Old Testament.

God's glory was like a white-hot, "consuming fire" on top of the mountain when the Lord gave Moses the Ten Commandments (Ex. 24:17). Moses was hidden in a crevice of a rock as the glory of the Lord passed by Him (see 33:22). And the glory of the Lord consumed the sacrifice and filled the tabernacle when it was completed (see 40:34-35).

The prophet Isaiah reflected God's desire for His own glory:

> Look, I have refined you, but not as silver;
> I have tested you in the furnace of affliction.
> I will act for my own sake, indeed, my own,
> for how can I be defiled?
> I will not give my glory to another.
> **ISAIAH 48:10-11**

God does many things, but behind them all is a commitment to His own glory. He saves for His own glory. He delivers for His own glory. He judges for His own glory. God always acts for His own glory, and this pursuit is not only good and right but also loving.

While any human being who acts in a self-glorifying way is rightly seen as egotistical, boastful, arrogant, and selfish, it's entirely appropriate for God to seek His own glory. That's because of all the beings in the universe, God is the only One who actually deserves the glory. So whenever we hold something higher than God in our hearts, we call that thing an idol. If God desired something other than His own glory, He would by definition become an idolater.

God's glorious name should be the driving force behind our prayers, just as it's the driving force behind all His actions. For that reason when we pray, we must ask God to bend our hearts to His ways, to create in us a greater love for His glory and His name so that we truly desire what He desires.

**Why is it important for Christians to love and lift up the glory of God?**

**In what specific ways do our prayers change when we desire God's glory?**

**Can you think of a specific time when you saw God glorify Himself through a painful circumstance? What happened?**

## PRAY

*Reread today's Scripture passages and turn them into individual prayers that seek a greater passion for God's name and glory. Pray that just as God's driving passion is His own name, He will give you an overarching passion for His glory as well.*

# DAY 4
## *The Saving Name*

**Read Acts 4:8-12.**

The name of God is holy. When we pray, we aren't praying for His name to be holy but for it to be recognized as what it already is. Part of recognizing God's holiness, however, is recognizing that we aren't holy.

If God is holy, meaning He's completely other than we are and perfect in every way, then how can we ever live in a right relationship with Him? How can we expect to come to Him in prayer and expect Him to welcome us? It's only through the gospel that we become acceptable to the holy God. In Christ we're given the great benefit of His righteousness even as He takes our sin on Himself. This is why the name of God is not just holy; it's also the only name under heaven by which we can be saved.

This was the declaration of Peter when he was questioned by the Jewish leaders in Jerusalem. The previous day when Peter and John healed a lame man outside the temple, they did so in the name of Jesus Christ of Nazareth (see Acts 3:6). They went on to declare to the amazed crowd that this healing demonstrated the power of God and that the people should repent of their disbelief. When the Jewish leaders called Peter and John before them to question them about the healing, Peter delivered this message about the saving name of Jesus:

> Rulers of the people and elders: If we are being examined today about a good deed done to a disabled man, by what means he was healed, let it be known to all of you and to all the people of Israel, that by the name of Jesus Christ of Nazareth, whom you crucified and whom God raised from the dead—by him this man is standing here before you healthy. This Jesus is
> the stone rejected by you builders,
> which has become the cornerstone.
> There is salvation in no one else, for there is no other name
> under heaven given to people by which we must be saved.
> **ACTS 4:8-12**

The name of Jesus is certainly recognizable. Indeed, there's no more recognized name throughout all of human history. Politicians, athletes, rulers, generals— all these have names that are remembered in some corner of the globe, but the name of Jesus stands apart from the rest. This name has stood the test of time, spanning geographical, economic, racial, and national barriers. The name of Jesus has universal appeal because it has the power to save.

When we trust in the name of Jesus, we declare that our hope is in who He is and in His saving work on the cross for us. When we pray for the name of God to be revered and for His glory to be revealed throughout the earth, we're also praying that more and more people will come to trust in the name of Jesus, for that name alone gives them the ability to approach a holy, glorious God.

**What are some other names people might trust in hopes of salvation?**

**Recall the time you realized you needed to be saved and you trusted in the name of Jesus. What emotions did you experience?**

**Record the name of one person you can pray for today to know the saving name of Jesus.**

## PRAY

*As you pray, speak the words of Acts 4:12 to Jesus, telling Him that there's no other name other than His by which we must be saved. Thank Jesus for saving you. Pray for the person you identified who needs to know the saving name of Jesus.*

## DAY 5
# *The Only Name*

**Read Philippians 2:1-11.**

Praying for God's name to be honored as holy can be discouraging. Perhaps you've begun to pray for a person, a circumstance, or an area of the world, asking the Lord for His name to be revered, respected, and trusted in that situation. But then your doubt takes hold.

You start to second-guess your prayer, recalling that the person you're praying for has heard the gospel many times before and has rejected it. Or your gaze shifts to that circumstance and you realize again how desperate it is, seemingly without hope of change. Or as you think about a region of the world, you consider the cultural or religious challenges to honoring God's name there. You can feel discouraged and even hopeless when you think about those circumstances and your desire for the name of God to be known and loved among those people and in those situations. In those moments we must remember that the desire to extend and honor God's name isn't merely a wish that Christians entertain; it's actually a promise.

Paul recorded in Philippians 2 a succinct, beautiful description of the character of Jesus. He reminded his audience of the nature of Jesus, who, though He's God, nevertheless humbled Himself even to death on a cross. Many scholars believe that the words in this chapter weren't original to Paul but that he borrowed them from an ancient Christian hymn guiding the early Christians to remember and love Jesus.

Paul closed this passage with a powerful declaration about the name of Jesus Christ, who is in very nature God:

> For this reason God highly exalted him
> and gave him the name
> that is above every name,
> so that at the name of Jesus
> every knee will bow—
> in heaven and on earth
> and under the earth—
> and every tongue will confess
> that Jesus Christ is Lord,
> to the glory of God the Father.
> **PHILIPPIANS 2:9-11**

Notice the definite nature of Paul's pronouncement: "Every knee will bow" (v. 10). "Every tongue will confess" (v. 11). Honoring Jesus Christ isn't in doubt. Indeed, the question isn't whether every person will bow down before the Lord Jesus; the only question is when it will happen for each one of us.

When we pray for God's name to be regarded as holy, then, we aren't merely wishing something to be true. We aren't just longing for a change of minds and perspectives around the world. We're laying hold of a great promise that frames the culmination of history. We're declaring that what God has said will come to pass: that Jesus Christ *will* be declared and acknowledged as the true King. His name *will* be revered. Because this is a promise, we can confidently pray in any and every situation, "May Your name be recognized and revered as holy."

**What's one situation you're confronting in which it seems impossible for the name of Jesus to be lifted up?**

**How does knowing that reverence for Jesus' name is guaranteed change the way you pray about that situation?**

**How have you seen God make His name great in seemingly impossible situations like this before?**

## PRAY

*In your prayer today express confidence that the name of Jesus Christ will be known and honored throughout the entire world. Based on that promise, confidently pray for the situation you identified. More than anything else, pray that God will be glorified in that situation.*

# THE KINGDOM AND WILL OF GOD

# START

Welcome to group session 3 of *Pray like This*. Ask participants to discuss what they learned in their personal study by answering the following questions.

**What's one truth that stood out to you as you completed the personal study this week?**

**As you focused on honoring the name of God as holy, did you notice any changes in your daily perspective?**

The next lines of Jesus' Model Prayer deal with the kingdom and the will of God:

> Your kingdom come.
> Your will be done
> on earth as it is in heaven.
> **MATTHEW 6:10-11**

**How would you define *kingdom of God?***

Just as Jesus pointed to the glory of God in the previous portion of His prayer, He continued with a God-centered perspective. Jesus instructed us to pray that God's kingdom would come and that God's will would be done on earth as it is in heaven. In this video session your group will discover more about the kingdom of God and why Christians should actively seek God's kingdom and God's will.

**Read together the text of Jesus' Model Prayer, found in Matthew 6:9-13. Then watch video session 3.**

# WATCH

God's glory and honor are directly tied to the matter of authority. God's name is to be hallowed because God is in charge.

God's kingdom is His rule and reign both in our lives and on the earth and one day on the new earth.

The kingdom comes in our lives when we are surrendered to the will of God, when we're dying each day to our own desires.

We pray for the kingdom of God to come and for the will of God to be done, and then we act in faith by doing the things that are tangible examples of the rule and the reign of God.

When we are asking for the kingdom of God to come in situations of life, then we're asking that the ruling presence of Jesus that already exists would exist in this very moment, for this very season, for this specific time in my life.

"Your kingdom come" and "Your will be done" are going to put you in the right posture of both petitioning in prayer as well as submission in prayer.

When we're praying for the kingdom of God to come, we are really asking God to make us instruments in a partnership with other people that are praying these same prayers to multiply the kingdom.

Sometimes it's difficult for us to understand or discern God's will because it is so different from what we think we want in the natural.

We're in essence asking God to bring to fruition and to its fullness what we already enjoy.

With the kingdom comes the King.

We want our prayer life to give us greater obedience, not greater hypocrisy.

It's very important that we connect our obedience and our prayers together so that our prayers are helping us to live things out.

# DISCUSS

Jesus told us that we should pray for God's kingdom to come and for God's will to be done on earth as it is in heaven.

**After watching the video, how would you define *kingdom of God*?**

**When we genuinely pray for God's kingdom to come and His will to be done, what's revealed about our hearts?**

**What's challenging about praying like this?**

The kingdom of God is present anywhere the reign and rule of God are lovingly embraced. The kingdom of God has already come in Christians because we've surrendered to His will as our Lord. We should continue to pursue God's will and rule in us and in the rest of the world. Of course, we must relinquish our own will and die to ourselves daily, for we can't pursue both our will and God's will at the same time.

**Why is dying to ourselves necessary for us to seek the kingdom of God?**

**What are some ways Jesus taught us—not only with words but also with actions—to seek the will and kingdom of God?**

**What practical actions can we take to show our commitment to the will and kingdom of God?**

As we pray, we pray in faith that God will bring His kingdom. One way we show the validity of our faith is through our actions, seeking the kingdom and the will of God even as we pray for them to come.

## PRAY

*Lead the group in prayer. Pray that you and your group will surrender your will to God daily. Pray that God will bring His kingdom and that you and your group will actively seek His kingdom.*

# DAY 1
# Embracing the Kingdom

**Read Luke 17:20-21.**

Having helped us, as His disciples, see the unique privilege of coming to God as our Father, Jesus then taught that our prayers should be dominated by a vision for the name and the glory of God. His next phrase has a similar theme:

> Your kingdom come.
> Your will be done
> on earth as it is in heaven.
> **MATTHEW 6:10-11**

This instruction is directly in line with the entire ministry of Jesus, for He frequently taught on the kingdom of God. The phrase *kingdom of God* is found in more than fifty separate sayings in the Gospels and in many more parallel passages. Jesus not only talked about the kingdom of God but also saw Himself as a messenger and the means of the coming of God's kingdom:

> Being asked by the Pharisees when the kingdom of God would come, he answered them, "The kingdom of God is not coming with something observable; no one will say, 'See here!' or 'There!' For you see, the kingdom of God is in your midst."
> **LUKE 17:20-21**

To Jesus, the kingdom is both a spiritual and a physical reality. It's the realm in which God's rule and reign are fully realized. Jesus, who not only preached the kingdom but also lived the kingdom, brought it to bear on earth. When we pray for and seek the kingdom of God "on earth as it is in heaven" (Matt. 6:11), it means we want to see the reality of joyful submission to God's rule and reign.

Spiritually, the kingdom is where we live by faith in Christ and fully give ourselves to the purposes of God. Physically, the kingdom is where we work to bring about justice, healing, and provision. We must pray and work to bring about both of these realities on earth. We share the good news of salvation in Christ, and we feed the hungry. We teach people to grow in intimacy with God, and we give shelter to the homeless.

But the very fact that we're to pray for God's kingdom to come and for His will to be done forces us to recognize that although Jesus brought the kingdom to the earth in Himself, the kingdom isn't yet fully realized.

The kingdom of God burst into the world in the person of Jesus Christ. He came in power, and His death on the cross conquered death. The end is no longer in doubt. Yet there are still battles to be fought. There's still a kingdom to be advanced. We have work to do in prayer, and we must do it until the day Jesus splits the sky and comes back again.

When we pray for God's kingdom to come and for His will to be done, then, we're praying for people to honor God through submission to Jesus as Lord and for the world's values to align with the priorities of God's kingdom. That means we pray for the lost to be saved, for the hungry to be fed, and for the helpless to be protected. In all these ways and more, God will continue to bring His kingdom and will on earth, even as it is in heaven.

**Why is it important to recognize the spiritual and physical natures of God's kingdom?**

**How specifically have you been praying for the kingdom of God to come and for His will to be done?**

**How does having a greater understanding of the kingdom of God help you pray for His kingdom to come and for His will to be done?**

## PRAY

*Before you begin to pray today, think about the nature of God's kingdom. Ask the Lord to give you a wholehearted desire to see His kingdom come on earth and for His will to be done. Then apply the prayer for His kingdom to specific situations you see around you and in the world.*

# DAY 2
# Understanding God's Will

**Read 1 Thessalonians 4:1-7.**

"What is God's will for my life?" Surely most Christians have asked this question. And surely they've done more than simply ask; they've prayed to know God's will. Most of the time when we ask the question, we want an answer to a specific issue in our lives. We want to know God's will about what job we should pursue, what city we should live in, or whom we should marry.

Jesus told us to pray that as God's kingdom comes on earth, His will would also be done. The accomplishment of God's will fits hand in glove with the coming of His kingdom, for it's in God's kingdom where His will is lovingly and joyfully obeyed. Though it's good and right for us to seek the answers to specific questions, the plain truth is that the vast majority of God's will has already been revealed to us. His Word is full of commands that reveal the way we should live and the way we should pray. Consider just one example from Paul's letter to the Thessalonians:

> This is God's will, your sanctification: that you keep away from sexual immorality, that each of you knows how to control his own body in holiness and honor, not with lustful passions, like the Gentiles, who don't know God.
>
> **1 THESSALONIANS 4:3-5**

In other words, we don't need to pray about whether it's God's will for us to be sexually pure; we know without a doubt that God's will for us, as for every Christian, is to be conformed to the image of Christ. It's His will that we should be pure and holy, living in a way that reflects our calling as His children.

The vast majority of us don't need further education on God's will; instead, we need to begin living more fully in what we already know God's will to be. This fact changes the shape of our prayers, both for ourselves and for others.

We can apply this line of Jesus' Model Prayer—for God's will to be done—on an individual level. Instead of spending most of our time praying to find out what God's will is, we might pray instead for courage and perseverance to live inside His revealed will. We might pray that we'll be pure. That we'll be faithful husbands and wives. That we'll lovingly and generously serve the church.

In the same way, we can confidently pray for others inside God's will. We can ask the Lord for our lost friends and family members to come to know Christ, for we know this is His will. We can pray against systemic injustice that we see around the world, for we also know that God's will is for justice to reign. We can pray for people in positions of power and authority, knowing that this is God's will too.

In short, when we read God's Word, we're reading His will, and that Word can inform us accordingly.

**Do you agree with the statement that we should focus our prayers on doing what we know is God's will rather than discovering what we don't know? Why or why not?**

**What are some specific elements of God's revealed will that you need to pray for courage to pursue?**

**How does embracing God's revealed will change the way you'll pray for the people closest to you?**

# PRAY

*Use the previous questions to guide your prayers today. Carefully consider what you know to be God's will for your life. First pray for yourself, then for others, according to God's will as revealed in His Word.*

# DAY 3
# Submitting to God's Will

**Read Matthew 26:36-46.**

Jesus gave us the words of the Model Prayer in response to a request from His disciples. They asked Him to teach them how to pray (see Luke 11:1), and that's exactly what the Model Prayer does. It's a lesson in prayer. But the Bible shows us more than this lesson; it shows us that Jesus practiced what He preached.

Jesus not only taught us how to pray but also showed us how to pray in various passages in the Gospels. Although the Bible tells us of many occasions when Jesus went off by Himself to pray, perhaps our most vivid picture comes from the night before His crucifixion. Knowing His death was imminent and knowing the suffering He would endure, Jesus approached His Father. The substance of that prayer involved the will of God.

The Bible tells us that during the night, Jesus was in spiritual anguish because of what was coming. He prayed to His Father, asking if there might be another way for His plan of redemption to come to pass. But ultimately, Jesus yielded to the wisdom and authority of His Father:

> Going a little farther, he fell facedown and prayed, "My Father, if it is possible, let this cup pass from me. Yet not as I will, but as you will."
> **MATTHEW 26:39**

Jesus submitted to the will of God even though He knew the pain, hardship, and suffering it would cause Him. Submission to the will of God would cost Jesus His life, and it's the same with us. When we pray for God's will to be done, we're implicitly stating that our will shouldn't be done. We're giving over our plans, our dreams, and our aspirations to the will of God. In a sense we're dying. Submission to God's will requires us to die to our will. Furthermore, Jesus told us it would be so:

> If anyone wants to follow after me, let him deny himself, take up his cross daily, and follow me. For whoever wants to save his life will lose it, but whoever loses his life because of me will save it.
> **LUKE 9:23-24**

If we want to follow Jesus, it will cost us everything. Just as the cross meant certain death for people who carried it during that time, taking up our cross today means we're giving ourselves over to death. It means every day we're willing to die to ourselves in order to live according to the will of God. This reality should make a forceful impact on us as we pray for the will of God to come to pass.

When we pray for God's will, we're committing ourselves to God's plans rather than our own. We're expressing trust in Him, believing we're dying to the path that might be most comfortable, profitable, or easy for us because it falls short of God's will for our lives.

So we pray for God's will to be done, recognizing that in doing so, we're giving ourselves over to Him. But we do so in faith, believing that those who lose their lives will once again find them in Christ.

**What's one specific situation in which you're struggling to trust God and His will?**

**In that situation what part of you must die for you to pray, "Your will be done"?**

**How does trusting God and His character enable us to pray like Jesus?**

## PRAY

*Think about the ways you answered the previous questions. Recognize that part of you must die for God's will to be done. Then willingly embrace that death as part of your prayer today. Pray for God's will to be done while recognizing the death to self that this prayer will require.*

# DAY 4
# Trusting God's Will

**Read James 4:13-17.**

Because God is sovereign, all the moments of our days are ordered. That's true even for a king:

> A king's heart is like channeled water in the LORD's hand:
> He directs it wherever he chooses.
> **PROVERBS 21:1**

Furthermore, God always acts in accordance with His will, and His will is good and perfect even though we, as humans, might not understand how or why He makes the decisions He makes. His ways are not our ways, nor are his thoughts our thoughts (see Isa. 55:8-9).

In our arrogance we might very easily assume a posture of presumption when it comes to the will of God. For example, we might assume what God's will is for our job, our finances, or our future without even asking Him about it. James warned against this kind of arrogance about the will of God:

> Come now, you who say, "Today or tomorrow we will travel to such and such a city and spend a year there and do business and make a profit." Yet you do not know what tomorrow will bring—what your life will be! For you are like vapor that appears for a little while, then vanishes. Instead, you should say, "If the Lord wills, we will live and do this or that." But as it is, you boast in your arrogance. All such boasting is evil. So it is sin to know the good and yet not do it.
> **JAMES 4:13-17**

In our limited ability to know what will come in the future, we can't make claims about what will happen next. As James said, we're like a vapor. Even our next moments of life aren't promised to us. Unlike us, God not only knows what will happen but is also exercising His sovereign power to bring it about. How should we respond to this reality?

On the one hand, we might live with a sense of fatalism. Concluding that nothing we do really matters because God has determined His will and will bring it about, we simply stop living. And we stop praying because we think our prayers won't affect the outcome God has already decided.

On the other hand, though, we might live with even more confidence. We might pray even more because maybe God has determined that our prayers will be the reason a certain circumstance changes. But to press on further in prayer, we must not only know that God's will is sure and certain; we must also trust that His will is the best outcome.

Fortunately for us, God's will is a function of His character. If we believe that God is good, loving, generous, and wise and that He's a Father who always acts in the best interests of His children, we should long for His will to be done. It's because we trust in the character of God, who has shown Himself to be faithful time and time again, that we can trust the will of God.

So even though we might not know what tomorrow holds and even though we can boastfully make claims about the future, we can nonetheless pray for God's will to come to pass. For Christians, then, praying for God's will to be done is both a matter of great humility and of great boldness at the same time.

**Is presumption creeping into any of your prayers? In what ways?**

**How does being limited in your knowledge of God's will fill you with humility and boldness at the same time?**

**What's one situation in which you're longing to see God's will done?**

## PRAY

*As you pray, evaluate the posture of your heart. Is pride lurking there? Are you making assumptions about God's will? Repent of these attitudes and confess to God that His will is always best. Ask the Lord to help you pray for His will to be done as an expression of confident humility.*

# DAY 5
## Kingdom Come

**Read Acts 1:4-8.**

The kingdom of God is an already-but-not-yet reality. Think of it like this. Two important historical dates marked the end of World War II. The first date is remembered as D-day—June 6, 1944. When the Allied powers stormed the beach at Normandy, they effectively broke the back of the Axis powers. By taking that beach, the Allies secured the victory, and it was just a matter of time until the war was over. However, the official war continued until May 7–8, 1945, when the Allied powers accepted the unconditional, full surrender of Germany. That's when the fighting completely stopped.

Almost a full year of fighting, shooting, and casualties took place between the time when victory was secured and the time when victory was declared. Although the victory was sure, there were still battles to be fought in the meantime.

Christians are living in that meantime in a spiritual sense. Jesus brought the kingdom with Him, and He secured the ultimate victory for God's kingdom through His death and resurrection. But that victory won't be fully realized until Jesus returns. In the meantime Christians are the representatives of the kingdom of God on earth. That means the values, priorities, and goals of the kingdom should be fully represented in the church. When people look at the church, they should see a visual representation of what the kingdom of God will be like when Jesus comes back.

When will that happen? We don't know, and Jesus isn't concerned that we know. Instead, He's concerned that we're busy with the work of God's kingdom, praying and working for it to come in power, right now in the meantime.

Days after the resurrection of Jesus, His disciples asked Him a question about the kingdom. They wanted to know whether Jesus was going to restore the kingdom to Israel at that moment (see Acts 1:6). The disciples still had a fundamental misunderstanding about the nature of God's kingdom. They were still thinking in political terms, and they wanted Jesus to restore the nation of Israel to its former status as a world power. Jesus' response redirected their focus from the timing of their idea of the kingdom to the work they should be carrying out before the kingdom would be consummated:

> It is not for you to know times or periods that the Father has set by his own authority. But you will receive power when the Holy Spirit has come on you, and you will be my witnesses in Jerusalem, in all Judea and Samaria, and to the end of the earth.
>
> **ACTS 1:7-8**

Jesus' followers today might easily be consumed with the timing of God's kingdom. We know someday Jesus is going to return, and His victory will be consummated here on earth. Yet He left work for us to do in the meantime. Rather than concerning ourselves with *when,* we should be concerned with *what.* Therefore, our prayers should focus on sharing the gospel in all corners of the globe and completing the mission Jesus gave to His followers. This is one more way we pray for the kingdom to come on earth as it is in heaven.

**How can a concern with the timing of God's answers to our prayers distract us from the kingdom work Jesus has given us to do?**

**How would your prayer life be different if you saw the work of the Great Commission as your primary focus in life?**

**Identify one person you pray will receive Christ. What's one area of the world in which you can focus your prayers for the gospel to spread?**

## PRAY

*Use recent news stories you've seen to guide your prayers for the gospel. Pray for the gospel to spread in the areas of the world that were mentioned in those reports.*

# THE PROVISION OF GOD

# START

Welcome to group session 4 of *Pray like This*. Ask participants to discuss what they learned in their personal study by answering the following questions.

**What's one truth that stood out to you as you completed the personal study this week?**

**What opportunities did you see in your life and your community for the kingdom of God to be advanced?**

Jesus next instructed us to ask God to "give us today our daily bread" (Matt. 6:11).

**Why do you think Jesus included this petition next?**

This week we see Jesus make a transition to personal petition. When we ask God to give us our daily bread, we're acknowledging some important facts about who God is and who we are. As we watch the video session, we'll come to understand some implications of this request.

**Read together the text of Jesus' Model Prayer, found in Matthew 6:9-13. Then watch video session 4.**

# WATCH

God wants us to be at home with Him, living in prayer.

We should pray as if everything depends on God.

We have needs because we live in this world, and this prayer acknowledges the reality of those needs, but it also acknowledges the reality that God is the provider.

God knows there's something we need greater than our daily needs, and that's an awakening to who He is—His power, His presence, His majesty, His will, His kingdom.

In asking, we're saying, "We recognize that we can't provide anything in and of ourselves. Only You can."

Jesus already knows what we ask before we even ask it.

When we ask God to give us our daily bread, in essence we're asking the Bread of life, who is our spiritual bread, to also be the avenue whereby we receive the physical bread that we need simply to live life in this world.

When we ask for daily bread, what we're saying is "God, You're the source of everything good in my life, and You've created my body with needs."

We're privileged to ask for everything we need for our provision that day.

God is teaching us that He's always enough for us.

I won't have bread for life apart from Jesus.

We can quickly convince ourselves that we actually are self-sustaining creatures.

One of the things that we can do in praying for our daily bread is to not live based on assumption, to pray and ask the Lord for simple things.

# *DISCUSS*

In His Model Prayer Jesus next told us that we should ask God to give us today our daily bread.

**What's one insight you gained from the video teaching this week?**

**What do we acknowledge about the character of God when we ask Him to give us our daily bread?**

**Why do you think Jesus told us this should be a daily request?**

God is our provider. Whether or not we recognize it, we're dependent on Him each day to give us everything we need. When we pray like this daily, we acknowledge that God alone can fulfill all our needs and satisfy us. We also humbly acknowledge that we can't provide for ourselves.

**How does praying like this view both God and ourselves in our proper places?**

**What are some ways you saw God provide everything you needed this week?**

**What are some barriers in your life that keep you from having complete trust in God as your provider?**

God can be trusted. We know this from our past experiences because He has given us everything we need. But we also know this because He has ultimately provided for our greatest need through the death and resurrection of Jesus.

## PRAY

*Lead the group in prayer. Pray that God will increase your faith so that you can trust Him for everything you need on a daily basis. Ask Him to give you a heightened sense of your need and His provision this week.*

# DAY 1
## The Bread from Heaven

**Read Exodus 16:1-20.**

Up to this point Jesus focused His Model Prayer on the name and glory of God and His kingdom. This emphasis is instructive for us because it reminds us that prayer isn't primarily about what we can gain but about the glory of God. Even when the Model Prayer shifts its focus to our specific needs, it does so by acknowledging our relative weakness and our need to trust God as our Provider.

In that light Jesus told us we should ask God, "Give us today our daily bread" (Matt. 6:11). Jesus used the metaphor of bread, the most basic provision for His audience, to say we should ask God to give us what we need to live and thrive in daily life.

This request recalls the time during the exodus when God provided for His people in the wilderness. Having been miraculously delivered from slavery in Egypt, the Israelites crossed the Red Sea under Moses' leadership. But despite witnessing the wonders of God, they soon drifted into fear and complaining:

> If only we had died by the LORD's hand in the land of Egypt, when we sat by pots of meat and ate all the bread we wanted. Instead, you brought us into this wilderness to make this whole assembly die of hunger!
> **EXODUS 16:3**

In response God provided what the people needed, giving them bread from heaven:

> I am going to rain bread from heaven for you. The people are to go out each day and gather enough for that day.
> **EXODUS 16:4**

The people soon found that God was very serious about the specific nature of His command, for when they gathered more than they needed, the bread from heaven bred worms and stank. This is a powerful lesson for both the children of Israel and the children of God today. When Jesus told us to ask for our bread and to do it daily, He was reminding us that only God can provide what we need.

In contemporary culture we've taken innumerable measures for our self-protection. Everything from insurance policies to refrigerators to 401(k)s to seat belts is meant to keep us safe. These things are intended to provide for our needs. None of these things are inherently bad, yet there's a danger similar to the one the Israelites faced when they gathered too much bread from heaven. When we hoard for tomorrow, we might quickly forget just how weak and needy we are.

So when we pray this portion of the Lord's Prayer, we're not only expressing our trust in God to give us what we need to survive; we're also acknowledging our own weakness and our dependence on God's gracious provision to give us life.

**What comes to mind when you think about your daily bread?**

**What are some specific ways God has provided for your daily bread in the past?**

**What forms of self-protection in your life or patterns of thinking might make you forget your daily dependence on the Lord?**

## PRAY

*In your prayer today verbally acknowledge your weakness and your dependence on God. Praise Him for His provision and His providential care for you. Then pray that He will supply the bread you need today.*

## DAY 2
# The Word of the Lord

**Read Matthew 4:1-11.**

When we ask the Lord each day to give us the bread we need each day, we're expressing confidence in His willingness and ability to provide what we need. We're simultaneously acknowledging our abject dependence on Him for the very fabric of our lives. God, as the great and generous giver, receives glory when He provides what we need.

But what do we really need? What's this bread we're praying for? Certainly it means the basic necessities of life like food, water, shelter, and even the breath in our lungs. And yet there's more, because as Jesus would teach us, we don't live on bread alone.

At the beginning of His earthly ministry, just after Jesus was baptized, the Spirit of God led Him into the wilderness specifically to be tempted by the devil. As in the garden of Eden, the tempter again came to a man—the Son of man. How would the second Adam respond to this temptation? Would He fall to His own human desires as the first Adam did, or would He respond in faith?

> The tempter approached him and said, "If you are the Son
> of God, tell these stones to become bread." He answered,
> "It is written: Man must not live on bread alone but
> on every word that comes from the mouth of God."
> **MATTHEW 4:3-4**

We shouldn't miss the fact that Jesus, having fasted for forty days and forty nights, was hungry. And a potential solution to His need for food was certainly within His grasp—to simply turn the stones to bread. But Jesus' response is a reminder that the daily bread we seek from the Father isn't merely physical; it's His Word that sustains us.

In fact, Jesus quoted the Word of God, Deuteronomy 8:3, in His response. There Moses had told the Israelites who had eaten the bread from heaven that God had given them the bread to remind them that their true and greatest need was spiritual, not physical. Such is the case with us.

When we come to God asking for our daily bread, we should be aware that our true need is in our souls. We need God and His Word to tell us who He is, who we are, the nature of life and the universe, and how we're supposed to live. As we pray for our daily bread, we can and should trust God to provide for us physically. At the same time, we should pray for and give thanks for His willingness to meet our greatest needs—the needs that go beyond physical hunger to the spiritual hunger for Him that all of us have.

**What place does the Word of God currently play in your prayer life?**

**Why does the nature of your prayers change when you realize that your greatest needs are spiritual and not physical?**

**Considering your spiritual need for God, what does it mean for you to ask Him for bread today?**

## PRAY

*As you pray today, give thanks to the Lord that through the gospel He has met your greatest need. Praise Him for doing what none of us could do for ourselves by sending Jesus to die in our place. Trust God to fill you not only physically but also spiritually.*

# DAY 3
# *The Day God Has Made*

**Read Psalm 118:19-24.**

No one knows for certain what today holds. This might be a day of great joy or immense sadness; it might be a day of opportunity or a day of rejection; it might be a day of laughter or a day of tears. We simply don't know for sure. How wonderful, then, to know that even though we suffer from an almost paralyzing lack of knowledge, the Lord knows our end before our beginning (see Isa. 46:10). Though we don't know what today holds, God certainly does.

How should we respond to that knowledge? In prayer we respond by confidently asking the Lord to give us what we need even though we don't know exactly what we need. But because we trust in His good character and correspondingly good provision, we can rejoice, for we're confident that this day, no matter what it holds, is the day God has made for us. This was the exhortation of the psalmist in Psalm 118:

> This is the day the LORD has made;
> let us rejoice and be glad in it.
> **PSALM 118:24**

This simple statement is full of great meaning for believers. Consider the implications of these few words.

First of all, "This is the day." It will do us no good to wish for another day, a different day, or the day someone else is having. This is the day we've been given. This day, full of the mundane and the ordinary, full of planned activities and unexpected opportunities, is the one we have.

Further, this is the day "the LORD has made." Regardless of what this day holds, it's the day the Lord has made. He isn't a cosmic clockmaker who set the universe in motion and then stood aside, watching it tick away. He's still in the business of making days, and He's made this one for us. Although we know very little of the potential ups or downs or highs or lows this day holds, it's nevertheless the one made by the Lord. And because He made it, we know He has also given us the resources we need for it. We have the grace we need, the patience we require, and the perseverance we find necessary. We have the discipline to do the work He has given us to do. Along with this day God has made,

He has also given us His limitless supply of resources, which we take hold of by faith when we ask Him for our daily bread.

"Let us rejoice and be glad in it." That statement doesn't mean everything today will make us happy and comfortable. Surely some things today will make us frustrated or sad, angry or disappointed. But this is the day the Lord has made. And because we know something about the nature and character of God, we can rejoice in this day, the one He has made for us, and be glad in it, trusting that though it might not feel like it at the time, everything that happens today has been filtered through the hands of a loving God.

Rejoicing in the day God has made means embracing the sovereign work of a loving God instead of wishing for another one. It means when we pray for our daily bread, we can do so with both joy and confidence.

**How does rejoicing in the day God has made show confidence in Him?**

**Is your prayer life filled with the kind of joy that should come with confidence in your Father? Why or why not?**

**What's one circumstance you're currently facing or are likely to face that's hindering you from rejoicing?**

## PRAY

*Remind yourself today as you pray, "This is the day the Lord has made." Express your confidence in God's will and plan, not just for your life as a whole but for the particular day before you. Choose in prayer to rejoice in what God has given you today.*

# DAY 4
## *The Secret to Contentment*

**Read Philippians 4:8-13.**

Bread is very basic in nature. For thousands of years, it has been one of the basic staples of life. But although bread provides what we might need for a given meal, it doesn't necessarily provide exactly what we want.

Consider the Israelites during the exodus. When the bread fell down from heaven, at first they were satisfied. But eventually, the bread grew boring to their taste buds, so they once again complained against Moses and the Lord:

> Why have you led us up from Egypt to die in the wilderness?
> There is no bread or water, and we detest this wretched food!
> **NUMBERS 21:5**

There's a considerable difference between what we need and what we want. When we pray, then, we should be careful not to assume that praying for God to give us our daily bread means trusting that He will fulfill every one of our wants in exactly the way we think He should. If that were the case, God would function more like a cosmic butler than a Heavenly Father.

Receiving our daily bread from God requires us to understand contentment. We must actively choose contentment when we consider God's provision, believing He has given us the right thing at the right time. That was Paul's point in Philippians 4:

> I have learned to be content in whatever circumstances I find myself.
> I know both how to make do with little, and I know how to make do
> with a lot. In any and all circumstances I have learned the secret of
> being content—whether well fed or hungry, whether in abundance or
> in need. I am able to do all things through him who strengthens me.
> **PHILIPPIANS 4:11-13**

Verse 13 is often quoted. We misunderstand its meaning, though, when we use this verse in a triumphant sense to claim that Jesus will help us conquer any foe or meet any challenge. The context indicates that Paul was specifically addressing the issue of contentment.

Here was a man, as he himself said, who knew what it meant to have little and to have plenty, to be well fed and to be hungry. And through Christ he could be content with whatever the Lord saw fit to give him on a given day. But we can't muster this kind of contentment on our own.

Our faith must be not only in God, who gives us our daily bread, but also in Jesus, who gives us strength to be content with God's provision. Through faith in Jesus and in His strength, we can accept the bread God gives us and be joyfully content with it at the same time.

**Are you currently struggling with contentment? Why or why not?**

**What does our contentment as Christians say we believe about God?**

**Why would a discontented heart eventually make it difficult to ask God to give you your daily bread?**

## PRAY

*The strength for contentment comes through Christ, so specifically pray today for a heart of contentment. Ask Jesus to give you strength to be content with your Heavenly Father's provision.*

## DAY 5
# *The God Who Provides*

**Read Philippians 4:14-20.**

Our God provides. That statement is straightforward enough, yet we still feel a measure of anxiety and worry when we think about the future. Will we have enough money? Will we get sick? Will we have a place to live? These are legitimate questions, yet we can take each one of them again and again to the Lord in prayer. And again and again we can ask the Lord to "give us today our daily bread" (Matt. 6:11).

We can trust God to provide. This was the testimony of Paul the apostle, the one who knew what it was to live with much and with little, to be well fed and to be hungry. Toward the conclusion of his letter to the church in Philippi, he wanted to emphasize God's ongoing provision, not just for his sake but for theirs:

> My God will supply all your needs according to his riches in glory in Christ Jesus. Now to our God and Father be glory forever and ever. Amen.
> **PHILIPPIANS 4:19-20**

This is indeed a bold claim, yet Paul was absolutely convinced of its truth. One reason for Paul's confidence was that he knew it wasn't hard for God to provide for His children. In these verses he reminds us that God has ample storehouses at His divine disposal for our needs. When He provides for us, He doesn't have to stretch Himself or take out a loan; He provides for us "according to his riches in glory" (v. 19).

Paul had no doubt about God's ability to provide for every one of our needs, no matter how extreme or dire they might seem to be in a given moment. But he wasn't confident only because He knew of the resources at God's disposal; he was confident because of what he had actually seen God do in the past.

We humans have incredibly short memories. Our pasts are littered with examples of instances when God provided for us in an ongoing way. Yet we either forget about those moments or never take time to reflect on exactly what God has done to give us the daily bread we need. If we stopped to consider, even just for a moment, all the times God gave us what we needed, our faith would be bolstered and emboldened.

True enough, He might not have given us everything we wanted. But in retrospect surely we can all point to specific times when His provision came from the most unlikely place—clear evidence of God's ongoing care for us as His children.

How then do we fight anxiety when we're worried about provision for the future? In prayer we can remember the storehouses of God, acknowledging that He doesn't lack anything and therefore has infinite resources at His disposal. At the same time, we can call to mind specific instances from our past when God provided in big and small ways. Having done these things, not only can we pray for what we need on a given day, but we can also do so with confidence in the God who gives the daily bread we need.

**What specific instances can you recall of God's provision in your life?**

**Which of these provisions came from unlikely places? Did you stop and thank God for His provision at the time?**

**How does remembering what God has done in the past help you pray with confidence about the future?**

## PRAY

*As you call to mind instances of God's provision, pause and thank God for each one. Acknowledge that in each case He provided what you needed at the time you needed it. Confess any occasions when you doubted the nature or timing of His provision. Then use these memories to help you pray for what you need today.*

# THE FORGIVENESS OF GOD

# START

Welcome to group session 5 of *Pray like This.* Ask participants to discuss what they learned in their personal study by answering the following questions.

**What's one truth that stood out to you as you completed the personal study this week?**

**Based on your study, why should we ask God for our daily bread?**

The next lines of Jesus' Model Prayer deal with forgiveness:

> Forgive us our debts,
> as we also have forgiven our debtors.
> **MATTHEW 6:12**

Jesus said we should ask God to forgive us as we have forgiven our debtors. Clearly, there's a link between our forgiveness of others and God's forgiveness of us. What's that link? And why should we pray for forgiveness if Christ has already forgiven us? This week's video session will help us discover insights into these questions.

**Read together the text of Jesus' Model Prayer, found in Matthew 6:9-13. Then watch video session 5.**

# WATCH

As we pray, it's good to remind ourselves that what we truly deserve is hell, but Jesus forgave us.

The grace you extend is tied to the grace you receive.

When I think about all that Christ did for me on the cross by taking my sins, bearing my shame, my guilt, in His body on that tree, how can I not forgive someone who's done something against me?

For us to ever come into the presence of a perfectly holy God and feel like we don't need forgiveness would be the greatest sense of arrogance.

Unforgiveness of others closes our ability to receive God's forgiveness.

Forgiveness is less about reciprocity. It's more about God's kindness to me.

One of the greatest sins in the church may be a lack of forgiveness, which stems from pride, and it stems from actually not preaching the gospel to ourselves.

It is God who releases us from the power of our past, the power of our sins.

When we take those wounds and those anxieties and those aches and need of forgiveness or need of giving forgiveness, it then brings us to a place of humility because all we can rest upon is grace.

No matter what somebody may have done to you, they have not done to you what your sin did to Jesus.

It's not that we forgive in order to gain God's forgiveness; it's that we forgive because we've been forgiven.

Jesus does not ask us to do anything that He's not. For me to truly identify with who He is—that He's a forgiving God—is for me to be able to step out in forgiving others.

When I freely and readily give you forgiveness, I am acknowledging, "How could I hold something against you that Jesus Christ, the King of the universe, has already let go?"

Jesus says you need to pray that way because what happens in your prayer life is manifested in your Christian life.

# DISCUSS

**What's one insight in the video that challenged you?**

**If God has already forgiven us in Christ, why must we continue to ask for forgiveness?**

**What are we acknowledging to be true about God's character when we humbly ask for forgiveness?**

When we ask for forgiveness of our sins, we're expressing faith in God's mercy. Our ongoing petition for forgiveness is an opportunity for God, again and again, to remind us of the good news of the gospel. It's also a chance for us, again and again, to humble ourselves before Him and declare that we need His mercy.

**Why did Jesus link our forgiveness of others with God's forgiveness of us?**

**What happens when we mentally disconnect that link?**

**Can you think of any other examples of Scripture in which these two avenues of forgiveness are linked together?**

**Can you share the names of any people you're struggling to forgive?**

Our willingness to forgive others reflects our understanding of God's forgiveness of us. If we have trouble extending forgiveness to another person, it might very well be because we aren't aware of the depth of our sin and the greatness of God's forgiveness of us.

## PRAY

*Lead the group in prayer. Ask members to silently ask for forgiveness. Encourage them to ask forgiveness for specific sins, not to pray a general prayer for forgiveness. Then pray for any members who confessed that they're struggling with forgiveness.*

# DAY 1
## The Condemned Sinner

**Read Romans 3:10-20.**

When we pray, we come into the presence of Holy God. This is a fearful prospect, for when we come into His presence, our sin is starkly exposed.

Time and time again in the Old Testament when people met with God, they assumed a humble and even terrified posture, not only because of God's power but also because in His presence they realized with vivid, startling clarity the depth of their sin. The holiness of God brings to light the sin of human beings. This is true without exception, for we are sinners without exception.

No one can stand in the presence of Holy God. No one can claim righteousness when they see what righteousness truly is. Any excuses or buts crumble in God's presence. There's no bartering or trading, for the only thing we bring into the presence of God is our own need—for provision, for care, but most profoundly for forgiveness.

Paul declared this truth in a universal way in Romans 3:

> All have sinned and fall short of the glory of God.
> **ROMANS 3:23**

It's no wonder, then, that Jesus taught that our pattern of prayer includes asking for forgiveness from God:

> Forgive us our debts,
> as we also have forgiven our debtors.
> **MATTHEW 6:12**

Asking God for forgiveness of our debts, or sins, isn't a one-time plea but a petition we make over and over again, for although we've been made righteous in Christ, we nonetheless commit acts of rebellion daily. We fail to live as the righteous sons and daughters God has declared us to be in Christ.

When we pray, then, we should make it our practice to ask for forgiveness. We should do so not only in a general sense but also specifically. We should confess specific instances of jealousy, anger, lust, lying, cheating, and every other way we've fallen short of God's holy standard.

We don't confess our sins to give God information. He knows better than we do the full extent of our sin. Nor do we confess our sins because God withholds His forgiveness until we ask for it. Once we've come into right standing with God through Christ and His sacrifice, God has forgiven our sins—past, present, and future.

We confess our sins to the Lord for the sake of our relationship with Him. God desires that we live in a love relationship with Him. He wants us to obey Him but to do so out of love for Him. Because we love God and because we know He loves us, we confess sin. We don't want anything, known but unspoken, to come between us and our Heavenly Father. We confess our sins so that our hearts can be unburdened and we can be reminded again of God's limitless, gracious love for us.

**When was the last time you truly confessed your sins to the Lord?**

**What benefit is there in confessing specific sins when we pray?**

**How does confessing your sins change the posture of your heart toward God as you pray?**

## PRAY

*Ask the Holy Spirit to bring to mind specific occasions when you've sinned. Confess these specific actions, thoughts, and feelings to the Lord. Ask for His gracious forgiveness for each one and thank Him for the sacrifice of Jesus, who died in your place for your sin.*

## DAY 2
# The Forgiving God

**Read Psalm 103.**

It's difficult to ask for forgiveness. When we know we've wronged someone, we're much more likely to remain silent and ignore the issue, hoping it will go away. Or when we eventually have the conversation, we often qualify our apology with buts and if onlys:

- I was going to do what I promised, but ...
- I would have been there if only ...
- I started to tell the truth, but ...

These kinds of qualifications nullify our apologies. These words reveal that we haven't yet truly owned our sin against the other person; instead, we're still trying to justify our actions or even push the blame onto someone else. Why do we do this?

Part of the reason is that it's inherently humbling to ask for forgiveness. When you truly ask for forgiveness, you're throwing yourself on the mercy of another person. You're confessing that you need something only they can grant, and it's entirely up to them whether to forgive you. In short, asking forgiveness removes the power of relationship from us and gives it to someone else.

This situation can be disconcerting because you don't know how the other person will respond. You don't know whether they'll be favorable and gracious or bitter and angry. They might assure you of their ongoing love, or they might tell you to keep your apology. Yet this ambiguity is one reason God's forgiveness is a powerful reminder of the gospel.

When we come to God, asking Him to forgive us when we've wronged Him, we can be assured of His response. We don't have to wonder whether we've outsinned His grace or overstayed our welcome in His family. We're secure in Christ, and based on the foundation of that security, we can know with glorious confidence how the Lord will respond when we humbly approach Him and ask for forgiveness.

The psalmist wrote about this reality in Psalm 103. The entire psalm reads as a tribute to our God, who forgives unceasingly and generously. In particular, verses 11-12 vividly describe the great extent of God's forgiveness:

As high as the heavens are above the earth,
so great is his faithful love
toward those who fear him.
As far as the east is from the west,
so far has he removed
our transgressions from us.
**PSALM 103:11-12**

When you come to God in prayer, you come knowing the way God will respond. So come often to the fountain of life-giving water (see Jer. 2:13), knowing that His mercy and forgiveness will never run dry.

**Why do you think asking for forgiveness is so difficult for some people?**

**Can you think of an occasion when asking for forgiveness has been particularly difficult for you? Why?**

**How does knowing God's response beforehand change the way you ask Him to forgive your sins?**

## PRAY

*Before beginning your prayer, read Psalm 103.*
*Pause after each section and reflect on the words.*
*Then let those words inspire your prayers for forgiveness*
*and your expressions of thanksgiving to God.*

# DAY 3
# The Honest Confession

**Read 1 John 1:8-9.**

Jesus' instruction in the Model Prayer to confess our sins reminds us that we always have sins to confess. The apostle John expressed it this way:

> If we say, "We have no sin," we are deceiving ourselves, and the truth is not in us. If we confess our sins, he is faithful and righteous to forgive us our sins and to cleanse us from all unrighteousness.
>
> **1 JOHN 1:8-9**

These verses contain both a universal truth and a powerful promise. The truth is that all of us have not only sinned but have also sinned recently. Even today. Perhaps in the last few minutes. This is because although we've been made new in Christ, the remnants of our old self remain. The pull of sin is strong and appealing, and far too often we choose to walk according to those sinful desires instead of walking according to the Holy Spirit who lives in us (see Rom. 8:5).

This is a universal truth. If we deny that we've sinned, John tells us we're delusional. We've tricked ourselves into thinking much more highly of ourselves than we ought. Further, we've begun to drift from a conscious need for Jesus and the cross in our lives. After all, if we don't have sin that grieves and offends our holy God, why do we need a Savior?

But these verses also contain a wonderful promise. As sure as the fact that we all sin is the fact that God is "faithful and righteous" (v. 9) to forgive us of that sin. When we humbly come to the Lord who loves us, having given His one and only Son as the substitute for our sin, we can know with certainty that He has forgiven us and will forgive us.

This universal truth and powerful promise bring us into a posture of humble honesty about our sin in prayer. Why would we hide? Why would we speak in generalities? And why would we hesitate to confess our sins to God? It's not as if we're telling Him anything He doesn't already know, for God already knows what we've done and the reasons behind it. In fact, He knows the facts in every situation better than we do.

Furthermore, we can be confident about God's response to our honest confession because He has promised to forgive us. Christians who ask the Lord to forgive our sins experience great freedom. When we humbly and honestly confess our sins, we not only receive God's pronouncement of forgiveness, but our hearts are also unburdened from the guilt that would result if we held on to the knowledge of our sins.

The ability to ask for forgiveness is God's gift to us. It's an opportunity for us to live freely as God declares again that He has released us from the burden of our sin. When we confess our sins with honesty, we can trust that our Heavenly Father will delight to tell us again what He has already done for us at the cross.

**Do you think you pray honestly when you ask for forgiveness? Why or why not?**

**Do you need to ask the Holy Spirit to help you pray more honestly about your sin? Explain why or why not.**

**Is anything else holding you back from honest confession in your prayers?**

## PRAY

*Ask the Holy Spirit to search your heart and to show you your most hidden sins. As He does, specifically and honestly acknowledge these transgressions, asking for the Lord's forgiveness. Thank Him for the sacrifice of Jesus, which assures you of the Father's forgiveness.*

# DAY 4
# *The Unlimited Pardon*

**Read Matthew 18:15-22.**

God's overwhelming willingness to forgive has great implications for believers. Because God forgives us without limit, we can live in freedom. We should want to please Him. Our lives should be filled with an ongoing sense of gratitude when we live in this forgiveness. But one of the strongest implications of God's forgiveness is our willingness to forgive other people.

Jesus knew this necessity well. That's why in the Model Prayer He linked God's forgiveness with our willingness to forgive others:

> Forgive us our debts,
> as we also have forgiven our debtors.
> **MATTHEW 6:12**

At first reading we might think Jesus was stating that God's forgiveness is proportionate to our forgiveness of others. But this prayer doesn't mean God will forgive us only when we forgive other people. It's saying that our willingness to forgive other people reflects what we perceive God's forgiveness of us to be like.

This is a difficult truth to grasp because we all love to be forgiven, yet we find it difficult to do the same when others have wronged us. It was certainly difficult for Peter, who pressed Jesus in Matthew 18 to learn the extent to which he had to forgive those who wronged him. Jesus had just finished teaching on the process of confrontation when a fellow Christian sins against us. Peter, hearing Jesus' emphasis on honest, direct communication with the aim of restoration, came back with what he considered a very generous offer:

> Lord, how many times shall I forgive my brother or sister
> who sins against me? As many as seven times?
> **MATTHEW 18:21**

Peter was hiding a statement in the form of a question. The rabbis of the day taught that three instances of forgiveness were sufficient. Peter went beyond that. He volunteered to forgive someone up to seven times, going well beyond what was culturally expected. But Jesus wiped the smugness off Peter's face with His next statement:

I tell you, not as many as seven, ... but seventy times seven.
**MATTHEW 18:22**

Jesus' point was clear: there's no specific limit to the number of times you should forgive another person; instead, you should generously forgive as God has forgiven you. This example helps us understand Jesus' emphasis in the Model Prayer. When we refuse to forgive others generously, we reveal that we don't truly understand and grasp the extent to which God has forgiven us.

Never should such a tragic error characterize us as believers. May we be people who mirror God's forgiveness to others. Because there's no limit to God's forgiveness of us, our forgiveness of others must be unlimited as well.

**How does confessing our sin to God help us forgive others?**

**Who's someone you're currently struggling to forgive?**

**What do you think is holding you back from extending forgiveness?**

## PRAY

*Thank God for the truth that there's no limit to His forgiving grace. Then pray specifically about forgiving the people in your life who've wronged you. Ask the Lord to remind you of how much you've been forgiven so that you can extend forgiveness to them.*

# DAY 5
# Forgiveness of the Forgiven

**Read Matthew 18:23-35.**

In Matthew 18 Jesus told a powerful story about the nature of forgiveness. He did so in response to a question from Peter about how many times we, as humans, needed to forgive others. Wanting to put a definite number on this forgiveness, Peter thought he was being generous by suggesting seven times. Jesus' response made clear that the issue wasn't a specific number of times but a heart that was always willing to forgive.

In the story that followed, Jesus illustrated where our unwillingness to forgive others comes from. In His story a servant owed a great debt to the king that he couldn't pay. Because he didn't have the means to pay his debt, everything he owned, along with himself and his family, would be sold into slavery. In response the servant threw himself on the mercy of his master, and "the master of that servant had compassion, released him, and forgave him the loan" (Matt. 18:27).

Because the debt was enormous, the forgiveness of it was extravagant. Yet the servant then went out to find a fellow servant who owed him a much smaller amount. Rather than following the example of his master, he violently demanded his payment in full, even throwing his fellow servant into jail due to his inability to pay.

When the master received word of what had happened, he was incredulous:

> You wicked servant! I forgave you all that debt because
> you begged me. Shouldn't you also have had mercy
> on your fellow servant, as I had mercy on you?
> **MATTHEW 18:32-33**

Jesus then forged the link between God's forgiveness and our willingness to forgive other people:

> So also my heavenly Father will do to you unless every
> one of you forgives his brother or sister from your heart.
> **MATTHEW 18:35**

Forgiven people forgive people. It's that simple. But the reverse is also true. When we find ourselves absolutely unwilling to forgive, it reveals that we don't comprehend the great debt of which God has forgiven us. Our lack of forgiveness shows that in our pride we don't consider ourselves to be truly in debt to God because our sin was either not that grievous or not that extensive. Nothing could be further from the truth.

Our sin cost Jesus His life. Our sin was so great that the required payment was the sacrifice of God's own Son. Knowing the devastating nature of our offenses, how could we withhold forgiveness from another person?

As we pray, we must pray with one eye on our own sin and one eye on our brother's. We must make sure we aren't so arrogant as to ask God for His forgiveness while we're withholding forgiveness from someone else.

**How does Jesus' story illustrate to you the link between God's forgiveness of you and your forgiveness of others?**

**How does an understanding of our personal debt to God motivate our forgiveness of other people?**

**In what ways can it be beneficial for you to regularly consider the great extent of your sin against God?**

## PRAY

*If you're struggling to forgive others, consider that you might have lost touch with the extent of the forgiveness you need. Ask God to mercifully remind you of your sin. Then give thanks for His forgiveness and ask Him to use that awareness to embolden you to forgive others.*

# THE PROTECTION OF GOD

# *START*

Welcome to group session 6 of *Pray like This.* Ask participants to discuss what they learned in their personal study by answering the following questions.

**What's one truth that stood out to you as you completed the personal study this week?**

**What would you say is the biggest benefit or blessing you've gained from this study?**

**What are some practical ways you sense God calling you to implement what you've learned in your prayer life?**

In this final session the group will discuss Jesus' concluding statement in His Model Prayer:

> Do not bring us into temptation,
> but deliver us from the evil one.
> **MATTHEW 6:13**

Both of these statements lead us to confront the real evil that's within us and around us.

**Read together the text of Jesus' Model Prayer, found in Matthew 6:9-13. Then watch video session 6.**

# *WATCH*

What God intends as a trial, Satan often intends as a temptation to sin. Satan's goal is to make you sin. God's goal is to help you grow in your discipleship and your sanctification.

The devil gets us to buy into the lie that this sin is OK because it's not a big sin.

As Christ followers, it behooves us not to emasculate evil.

The devil tempts us in basically three ways:

1. Lust of the flesh     2. Lust of the eyes     3. Pride of life

Being delivered from the evil one day by day is really just a foreshadowing of the fact that in the gospel God has already delivered us from evil.

There are three forces in this world that are affecting us as believers:

1. The devil himself     2. The world     3. The flesh

If I'm sensitive to the Holy Spirit, He reveals to me any unconfessed sin in my life so that I can be forgiven and walk blamelessly with the Lord.

If it's not for God's protective, prevenient grace with me, I will destroy my life.

God, I need You to save me from myself, and if it's not for Your grace in my life, then I would be doomed, but Your grace is dependable.

God is not an absentee landlord. He is Lord, and He is on that field with me in my struggle.

God makes us to be warriors, and He made us for the battle.

# DISCUSS

**What's one insight in the video that challenged you?**

**Why should we pray that God won't lead us into temptation?**

**If we're confronted with temptation, should we blame God for leading us into that situation? Why or why not?**

**What are some ways we can actively express our faith that God will answer this prayer?**

God's commitment to our good and our growth into the image of Jesus is sealed by the Holy Spirit in our lives. His will is for us to grow in holiness. Therefore, we must trust that God won't lead us into temptation. Further, when we're tempted, we should remember that the desire for sin still lurks inside us.

**Why is it important to be aware of the enemy in the world?**

**What stance should a Christian take toward the devil and his work?**

**How can praying like this make us more aware of the devil and his schemes around us?**

Christians should be aware but not fearful of the devil because God has already won the ultimate war through the death and resurrection of Jesus. When we pray for God to deliver us from evil, we're reminded that God is all-powerful and that Jesus has already defeated the enemy.

## PRAY

*Lead the group in prayer. Pray that God won't lead you into temptation and that He will deliver you from the evil one. Ask the Lord to help you recognize the evil inside your heart and the real presence of the enemy in the world.*

# DAY 1
## The Temptation of Doubt

**Read Genesis 3:1-7.**

Temptation is as old as the garden of Eden. Although we live in very different times from our first ancestors, the core of our temptations remains the same. Temptation, at the very heart, isn't specifically about sex, power, substances, or lying. At its root temptation is really about trust. At the heart of every temptation is a simple question that must be answered: Can God really be trusted?

Think back to those first moments in the garden. Everything existed in perfect harmony, and everything worked exactly the way God had designed it. There was no want, no dissatisfaction, no unmet expectations, and at the center of all this perfection was an unbroken fellowship between God and humanity. God and His created humans walked together in the garden, fully enjoying one another. Then came the temptation:

> Now the serpent was the most cunning of all the wild animals
> that the LORD God had made. He said to the woman, "Did
> God really say, 'You can't eat from any tree in the garden'?"
>
> **GENESIS 3:1**

The question seems simple enough, yet the cunning nature of the serpent was revealed in the subtlety behind the words. The serpent was doing much more than asking the woman a question; he was leveling a charge at the character of God.

With his question the serpent was challenging the generosity and love of God as the provider. If God really loved the man and the woman, why was He holding back something from them? Surely if He loved them, He would also give them access to the tree of the knowledge of good and evil. Furthermore, if God was really generous, He would want them to have the very best, and clearly, He didn't want them to have something this tree could provide.

While the particular objects of temptation may have changed over the years, the charge against God is still the same. And the temptation still begins with someone who doubts whether God and His ways can really be trusted. At the core, then, temptation is not only about our willpower to say yes or no at a given moment but also about whether we truly believe God loves us and has our best interests in mind when He gives His commands.

Like our ancestors in the garden, we're weak people. Offered an opportunity to doubt God in the face of temptation, we usually give in to that doubt. We would be wise, then, to recognize our weakness and practice praying as Jesus taught us:

> Do not bring us into temptation,
> but deliver us from the evil one.
> **MATTHEW 6:13**

It would be better not to be tempted at all so that the seed of doubt doesn't begin to grow.

**In your own words why is it important to pray that God won't lead us into temptation?**

**How does recognizing that our trust in God is at stake change the way you look at being tempted?**

**In what specific ways are you likely to be tempted today? How does that recognition change the way you pray?**

## PRAY

*Confess your weakness to God as you begin to pray today.
As Jesus instructed, ask the Father not to lead you into temptation.
Confess what you know to be true about God: that He's kind,
generous, and loving. Pray that He will help you remember
those truths when you're tempted to doubt His will and His ways.*

# DAY 2
## The Temptation Birthed

**Read James 1:2-15.**

Testing is valuable. Whether in the realm of physical fitness, academic aptitude, or spiritual maturity, tests are valuable for two reasons. First, testing reveals the quality of what's already present in a person. For example, a test in a class-room shows how much knowledge an individual has learned. Second, a test is valuable in developing a person. For example, muscles never develop unless they are regularly tested.

Similarly, the Book of James shows the value of testing for our spiritual growth. We're instructed:

> Consider it a great joy, my brothers and sisters, whenever you experience various trials, because you know that the testing of your faith produces endurance. And let endurance have its full effect, so that you may be mature and complete, lacking nothing.
> **JAMES 1:2-4**

Only through the testing of our faith do we grow into maturity. This purpose of tests is one God used throughout the Bible and continues to use in our lives today. However, the evil one can corrupt such testing, as James pointed out:

> No one undergoing a trial should say, "I am being tempted by God," since God is not tempted by evil, and he himself doesn't tempt anyone. But each person is tempted when he is drawn away and enticed by his own evil desire. Then after desire has conceived, it gives birth to sin, and when sin is fully grown, it gives birth to death.
> **JAMES 1:13-15**

Although God may allow His people to be tested, He does so only with our good and maturity in mind. But the evil one can take such trials and use them for his wicked purposes. According to James, the evil one works with our evil desires to corrupt this opportunity to grow and mature, using it as an opportunity to sin.

This is a sobering thought for all Christians, for it reveals the fact that temptation doesn't come only or even primarily from somewhere around us but from inside our own hearts. Corruption lives inside us; the old self that died when we came into Christ still lurks there, waiting for an opportunity to express the ways of the flesh (see Eph. 4:22-24). When we face temptation, we must recognize that our own hearts have put us in that position.

James clearly described the progression that's at work here. Something or someone comes into our field of vision. Our hearts entice us to use that person or thing for our selfish desires and perceived needs. But even at this point there's still time to resist temptation. We can choose whether to nurse and feed that temptation or to simply turn away. If we choose to feed our desire, it will eventually grow to consume us as we give in to sin. And finally, sin leads to death.

As we pray for God not to lead us into temptation, we should be aware that temptation doesn't come just from external sources. We need to remain aware of what we're already capable of that arises from our own hearts.

**Why is it dangerous to think of yourself as being above a certain temptation or sin?**

**Why is it important to recognize that God doesn't tempt anyone?**

**Why is it important to accept the fact that we're enticed to sin by our own evil desires?**

## PRAY

*As you pray today, confess the desires that lurk inside your heart. Acknowledge your weakness before God, praying that in light of that weakness, He won't lead you into temptation. Ask for courage to embrace the work of the Holy Spirit, who lives in you to help you resist temptation and to make you more like Jesus.*

# DAY 3
# The Temptation Avoided

**Read 1 Corinthians 10:6-13.**

Faith without action is dead. That is, faith is more than words or a feeling of certainty that God will come through in the end. When we pray, there are other ways besides verbal confirmation to testify that we believe God will respond. For example, we might pray for a friend to have his financial needs met, but maybe God has chosen to answer that prayer through our financial involvement. We might pray that a sick loved one won't feel alone, but maybe God has chosen to answer that prayer through our presence.

When we pray that God won't lead us into temptation but will deliver us from the evil one (see Matt. 6:13), the actions we take reveal the extent to which we trust God to do what we ask. In writing to the church in Corinth, Paul discussed temptation and identified a way can put into action our faith in God:

> No temptation has come upon you except what is common to humanity. But God is faithful; he will not allow you to be tempted beyond what you are able, but with the temptation he will also provide a way out so that you may be able to bear it.
> **1 CORINTHIANS 10:13**

When it comes to temptation, we aren't alone. As Paul reminds us, no matter how great our temptation might seem at a given moment, it's common to all humanity. We aren't the first or the last to face such a temptation. In addition, the temptation isn't more than we can bear, for God, in His faithfulness, will give us a way out.

This is where our action connects with our faith as we pray that God won't lead us into temptation but will deliver us from the evil one. We know by faith, then, that God isn't tempting us. Furthermore, we recognize by faith that God always provides a way for us to bear the temptation. The action we need to take is simple: we look for and take the way out that God provides.

If we're dealing with temptation by praying and expecting God to simply remove it from our lives, we aren't putting our faith into action. We aren't obeying God's Word in 1 Corinthians 10. Instead, we're taking a passive stance toward our temptation, playing the part of the victim who, in the end, might very well blame God for not taking the temptation away.

A biblical approach to addressing temptation is to recognize the reality of temptation and not be surprised when it comes. We can pray about the temptation, but along with our prayers we put our faith into action by actively looking for the particular way out that God has provided. We don't passively sit in the middle of temptation; we express our trust in God's provision of a way out by actively removing ourselves from the situation.

When we pray, we must recognize that our faith in God's willingness and ability to answer our prayers is measured not by our words alone but by what we do next.

**Can you think of a particular temptation in which you saw God provide a way out?**

**What factors keep you from actively looking for and then taking the way out of temptation that God provides?**

**What's one situation in which you know you'll be tempted today? What can you do now to help you respond to that temptation in a God-honoring way?**

## PRAY

*Pray today that the Lord won't lead you into temptation. Also pray about the specific situation you listed in which you know you'll be tempted. Ask the Lord for discernment to recognize the way out He has provided and for courage to walk in it.*

# DAY 4
# The Temptation Fought

**Read Matthew 4:1-11.**

At its core, temptation is a question of faith. When we're tempted, the root issue is whether God can really be trusted. Does He really love us? Is He really generous? Is He good? Is He really able to provide? Our response to temptation always comes down to our trust in God and His character.

Therefore, the way we fight temptation is by reminding ourselves again and again of who God is and then acting accordingly. So how do we know who God is? Thankfully, we aren't left to speculate about who God is, for He has written it down for us. We know who God is because of His Word.

God's Word is His revelation of Himself. He hasn't left us without a testimony of His will and ways, and He wants us to know Him. God's Word is the means by which we can know Him. For that reason it's also our weapon for fighting temptation.

In Ephesians 6 Paul described the spiritual armor that's available to every Christian. He described the helmet of salvation, the breastplate of righteousness, the shoes fitted with the gospel of peace, and other defensive pieces of armor. Yet there's only one offensive weapon at our disposal: "the sword of the Spirit—which is the word of God" (Eph. 6:17).

When we pray for God to "deliver us from the evil one" (Matt. 6:13), we do so with the weapon of our deliverance in our hands. There's no more powerful example of how this sword should be wielded against the forces of temptation than the example of our Lord Jesus. As He began His earthly ministry, He was led into the desert in order to be tempted (see Matt. 4:1-11).

Having fasted for forty days and forty nights, Jesus had a series of encounters with the devil. Each temptation was an effort to make Jesus compromise on what He knew to be true about His identity and His mission, but on a deeper level each temptation was about whether Jesus really trusted His Father—whether God's plan of redemption was really the right one. How did Jesus fight so great a temptation? With the Word of God.

With each temptation Jesus quoted from God's Word. He beat back the temptations from the enemy with God's truth. Consider that for a moment. The living Word of God used the written Word of God to obey the will of God.

Jesus taught us how to use the sword of God's Word. We would do well to look to His example and prepare ourselves for the battles that are inevitably coming our way.

When we pray, then, we ought to pray with the Word of God open. We should pray the promises of God and the statements about His character to Him, knowing that doing so conditions our hand to wield this mighty weapon.

**Does it surprise you that Jesus used God's Word to fight temptation? Why or why not?**

**How does reminding yourself of who God is serve as a weapon when you battle temptation?**

**How do your current knowledge of and commitment to God's Word reveal how important you believe it to be?**

# PRAY

*As you pray today, thank God for His Word. Ask Him to teach you how to use His Word to battle temptation. Pray that He will help you fight the temptations that will come your way today with the promises in His Word.*

# DAY 5
# The Temptation Conquered

**Read Romans 8:31-39.**

Conflict is difficult. Whether it's conflict at work, in a friendship, between parents and children, or in a marriage, hardly anyone relishes a fight. When we know conflict is coming, we often prepare ourselves emotionally, steeling our minds and hearts for the battle ahead.

For Christians, however, one type of conflict is never bad news. Paul described it:

> I say then, walk by the Spirit and you will not carry out the desire of the flesh. For the flesh desires what is against the Spirit, and the Spirit desires what is against the flesh; these are opposed to each other, so that you don't do what you want.
>
> **GALATIANS 5:16-17**

A conflict rages inside every Christian. When we're born again into Christ, we're made new; we're given a new heart, new tastes, a new identity, and new affections. And yet the old self won't go quietly. An internal battle continues between the flesh and the Spirit of God inside us. It's fought on a myriad of battlefields, both big and small, both visible and invisible. And you know what it feels like.

You know the pull of sin. The empty promises of satisfaction. The appeal of desire for immediate gratification. You know the inclinations of the Holy Spirit toward truth, goodness, humility, and holiness. And you know the internal tug-of-war very well. It's conflict in its purest form, and for believers, this conflict is good news.

Consider for a moment what the very presence of that fight inside you means. It means God hasn't given up on you. It means He's committed to making you more like Jesus. It means the Holy Spirit of God is alive and well in you, fighting for your sanctification. It means your faith is real.

This fight is painful. This fight is hard. This fight will continue as long as you're on earth. But this fight is good news. But there's even better news to come, for this conflict is temporary.

There will come a day when we'll no longer need to ask the Lord not to lead us into temptation. There will come a time when we'll no longer have to pray that He will deliver us from the evil one. For there will come a day when temptation and the evil one are vanquished. On that day the children of God will see the Lord face-to-face, and all the deepest desires of our souls will be fully realized in Him and in Him alone.

For Christians, in the meantime this means we pray and fight from a posture of victory. Though it might not feel like it during the heat of the battle, Jesus has already won the war. When we pray, then, we can pray with confidence, knowing that Jesus is our conqueror. And ultimately, we're conquerors along with Him.

**How would your prayer life change if you prayed from a resolute posture of victory in Christ?**

**What's keeping you from doing so?**

**As you pray, in what specific ways can you remind yourself that Christ has already won the war?**

## PRAY

*Thank God that Jesus has already won the ultimate victory. Ask the Lord to fill you with humble confidence in Him as you face temptation. Pray that the Lord will remind you daily of His great victory that you're blessed to enjoy.*

# WHERE TO GO FROM HERE

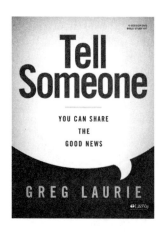

Discover the simple joy of evangelism as the good news of Jesus naturally overflows into your daily life. (6 sessions)

Gain a comprehensive understanding of religious liberty—and why it matters—as it relates to culture, the Bible, and the Great Commission. (6 sessions)

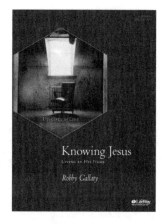

Explore the Gospel of John and move toward a more intimate relationship with Jesus through His miracles, what He said about Himself, and what others said about Him. (6 sessions)

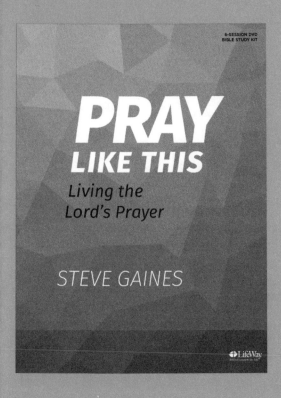

We hope you enjoyed *PRAY LIKE THIS*. Now that you've completed this study, here are a few possible options for your next one from some of the contributors to this one.

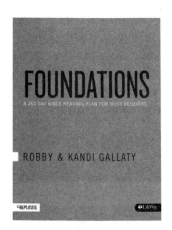

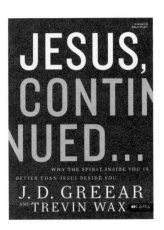

Learn how to Highlight, Explain, Apply, and Respond to key Bible passages through this one-year, five-day-a-week Bible reading plan.

Go beyond the doctrines you already know and see how you can have a satisfying, powerful relationship with God through the Holy Spirit. (8 sessions)

See how the gospel compels followers of Christ to counter culture on a wide variety of social issues in the world around them. (6 sessions)